CHILDREN IN CELL MINISTRY

Children in Cell Ministry

Discipling the Future Generation Now

JOEL COMISKEY, PH.D.

www.joelcomiskeygroup.com

Copyright © 2016 by Joel Comiskey

Published by CCS Publishing
23890 Brittlebush Circle
Moreno Valley, CA 92557 USA
1-888-511-9995

All rights reserved. No part of this publication may be reproduced, stored in a retrieval system, or transmitted, in any form or by any means, electronic, mechanical, photocopying, recording, or otherwise, without the prior written permission of the publisher.
Printed in the United States of America.

Cover design: Jason Klanderud
Editor: Scott Boren

ISBN: 978-1-935789-69-7
LCCN: 2015935354

All Scripture quotations, unless otherwise indicated, are from the Holy Bible, New International Version, Copyright ©1973, 1978, 1984 by International Bible Society. Used by permission.

CCS Publishing is the book-publishing division of Joel Comiskey Group, a resource and coaching ministry dedicated to equipping leaders for cell-based ministry.
Find us on the World Wide Web at www.joelcomiskeygroup.com

PRAISES FOR CHILDREN IN CELL MINISTRY

"Joel Comiskey's cry for the priority of the children in the Christian community echoes the passion of Jesus, Himself, and it cannot be ignored. He offers Biblical foundations, practical paradigms, and present day examples of what happens when a church takes its children seriously. While he sees the family as being the first and finest arena for children to grow into spiritual maturity, he recognizes that it happens best in a church culture which supports the parents and provides the resources of the community to equip the children. Though written in the cell church context, its message is to every church. It's hard to put this book

down without asking questions of ourselves. The issues call us to prayer and the Father's direction."
—**Dr. Lorna Jenkins,** *pioneer of children in cell ministry, prolific author*

"God has given a special gift to the contemporary Body of Christ by anointing Joel Comiskey to write this book. He reveals how to form cells with, and for, the precious children. It is the pioneer volume that exhaustively explains the theology and practice of children's cell groups. It is packed with examples of ways cell churches have successfully formed them in different cultures. The way to launch them is carefully explained."
—**Dr. Ralph W. Neighbour, Jr.,** *author, professor, and church planter*

"There is a big move of God going on among the children today. Thousands of children are being saved through children´s small groups. I praise God for this book, because it demonstrates this fact through testimonies and documented true stories from various churches that understood that they can form children into thousands of disciples of Jesus when they start this work in their childhood. This book is an invitation for parents, pastors, and leaders to meet and participate in this move of God"
—**Pastor Marcia Silva,** *founder and leader of children's ministry at the Vine Church, Goiânia, Brazil*

"Dr. Comiskey excels as a researcher. You have, in this book, a complete view about what is being done in cell churches around the world in this so important segment in church life. Children are the church of today. Every pastor, leader, and parent should read it and learn from a variety of children's ministries in different cell churches in this wonderful research. The cell world has truly been blessed and enriched by this masterpiece. Read it, meditate on its content, get inspired, and let yourself be impacted and transformed."

—**Robert Lay,** *founder and president of Igreja em Celulas, www.celulas.com.br*

"In such a time as this, we cannot neglect a generation who the enemy is trying to destroy. It must be our opportunity, challenge and primary concern to prepare them "for such a time as this." I pray this book is not just read - but that its fruit will be seen in the lives of the children who the readers come into contact with."

—**Daphne Kirk,** *author and founder of Generation to Generation, www.daphnekirk.org*

TABLE OF CONTENTS

Praises 5
Acknowledgements 11
Introduction 13

Chapter 1: Prioritizing the Future 21
Chapter 2: A New Vision for Children 33
Chapter 3: Simple Structure for the Vision 41
Chapter 4: Intergenerational Cell Groups 55

Chapter 5: The Nuts and Bolts of IG Cells 67
Chapter 6: Children Only Cell Groups 91
Chapter 7: Equipping The Children 119
Chapter 8: Equipping The Parents 143
Chapter 9: Cultivating The Vision 163
Chapter 10: Vision Mistakes 175
Chapter 11: Vision Focus 191

Endnotes 197
Resources by Joel Comiskey 207
Index 219

ACKNOWLEDGEMENTS

I'm very grateful for those who have made this book much, much better.

Scott Boren, my primary editor, helped me understand the big picture. He took a very rough draft and wisely guided me to reorganize the material. He suggested new chapters and helped me to rearrange the content. His expertise guided me throughout the process, and I'm grateful for his help.

Anne White took one month to thoroughly copy-edit the book. She has an expert eye for detail and found many inconsistencies in my grammar. She also thoughtfully pointed out weak arguments, and I'm very thankful for her faithful help.

Jay Stanwood's specialty is untangling complicated sentences and suggesting simple, straightforward solutions. Once again, he gracefully offered suggestions on how to make my sentences more understandable, and I appreciate his volunteer help.

Bill Joukhadar has a knack for finding errors that no one else notices. I'm very thankful for his eagle eye and sacrificial time spent on this book.

Rae and Charmaine Holt gave me concise, big picture advice on several aspects of this manuscript. Their deep knowledge of cell church and pastoral ministry helped them suggest some important changes. They also wisely pointed out errors throughout the manuscript.

John and Mary Reith have a gift of encouragement. They looked at the manuscript and gave gracious encouragement to me. It's a joy to read their comments.

Patricia Barrett pointed out specific errors and made important suggestions. I'm thankful for her help.

INTRODUCTION

In 2002 a five-year-old boy named Carlos came to Marisol's home cell group—one of the hundreds of Elim's children's cell group meetings in neighborhoods throughout San Salvador, El Salvador. Although he was only a child, Carlos was rebellious, disturbed the other children, and created havoc in the group. Marisol was patient and continued to invite Carlos to the group, gently correcting his discipline problems.

The other children told Marisol not to invite Carlos because his family was involved in crime. The parents of the other children also warned her that if Carlos continued to attend the group, they would not allow their children to go to the cell.

Marisol felt Carlos's behavior was a product of his desire to attract attention, so she decided to visit Carlos's family to know what was happening. When she arrived at Carlos's home, she found out that his father had abandoned him and that he had grown up with his mother, who was now in prison for theft. Carlos was now living alone with his older brother and another twelve-year-old boy who was part of a violent gang. Marisol also learned that Carlos had two uncles who were killed in gang violence. Neighbors said Carlos's family was under a curse.

Marisol decided to stand-up for Carlos and continued inviting him to the cell. Some parents stopped sending their children, wanting to avoid exposure to him. Marisol continued praying and ministering to him, warning Carlos not to follow the example of his brothers, but to follow Jesus and the Bible. Carlos eventually received Jesus as his Savior.

Slowly, Christ began to change Carlos and as Marisol observed those changes, she allowed him to lead parts of the group. As he assumed more responsibility, his behavior changed even more. As the years passed, Carlos grew in faith and his character became more Christ-like. Eventually, he joined a youth cell and was baptized in water. Carlos is now eighteen years old. He loves Jesus, is respectful of others, and has graduated from high school, something that no other family member has ever accomplished. He currently plans on studying physical education at the University of El Salvador with the goal of becoming a P.E. teacher.

Children, like Carlos, are being transformed throughout El Salvador through Elim's children's cell ministry. Mario Vega, the lead pastor of the Elim Church, said, "If children are not our present focus, the church has no future."[1] The goal of Elim is to develop more people like Carlos and change the culture of El Salvador in the process.

Books and seminars abound on small group dynamics, multiplication, coaching, church planting, and many other cell topics. Yet, the focus usually lies on adult ministry and the discussion of children takes a back seat—or is not discussed at all. Children are the silent majority that can't argue their case and are often overlooked because they are not a source for revenue or immediate church leadership.

This needs to change.

When I do seminars around the world, I have mainly talked about how cells apply to the adults. I might get one or two questions about children in cell ministry, but it has not been my main focus.

I have needed to change.

As you read this book, I hope that you will envision a new place, a new role for children's ministry, and that you will be able to say, "My church needs to change. We need to prioritize children."

PERSONAL JOURNEY

I have been writing about cell church themes since 1998, doing world-wide seminars on cell ministry, and coaching pastors. Inevitably, pastors and leaders want to know what to do with the children. I normally direct them to the writings of Daphne Kirk, Lorna Jenkins, or to an effective church that has excelled in children's cell ministry. Writing this book, however, has helped me to draw from other sources and dig deeper into the foundations for this important topic.

My own personal experience with children's cell groups began in Ecuador in 1998. It was during that year that my church transitioned to become a cell church, and implemented both intergenerational cell groups (children participating in the adult cell but having their own lesson time) and children only cell groups (adult-led children's groups that met apart from the normal adult cell).

The church hired a Christian education director, who became the supervisor or coach of the children's cell leaders. She prepared the material for children's cell groups that met in different homes throughout Quito, Ecuador. The same C.E. director was in charge of preparing the volunteers who ministered to the children during the Sunday celebration gathering.

In 2003, I planted a church in California which began with a single cell group. My children were intimately involved in our intergenerational cell group, staying in the adult cell for the icebreaker and worship time and then going into another room for their own Bible lesson. My wife would teach our children how to lead their lesson and then we would both coach them afterwards. All three of my children eventually led a kid's group, and two of them also led youth cells as the church grew. I saw firsthand that involving my own children at a young age prepared them for later leadership and ministry.

My personal experience has opened my eyes to the importance of this topic and sent me on a path of rethinking cell groups, the church, and the place of children in God's kingdom. By God's grace we have pioneers who have cleared a path for us to follow and provided inspiration for the content of this book.

PIONEERS

Lorna Jenkins was one of the early pioneers of children's cell ministry. In 1995 she wrote a manual, *Feed My Lambs,* and then in 1999, she wrote her classic book, *Shouting in the Temple,* which details how children's cells became a vital part of the Faith Community Baptist Church (FCBC) in Singapore. She also developed a plethora of equipping material, which I will highlight in a later chapter. Lorna Jenkins worked closely with Ralph Neighbour and Laurence Khong to place children at the heart of FCBC's cell transition. She excelled in connecting the children's teaching on Sunday with the home cell group material, which she provided to each cell group. She perfected the Intergenerational Cell group (IG group), during which children mixed with parents during the cell icebreaker and worship time, and then went to another room in the house to receive their own lesson. Adults in the cell group would rotate in teaching the children. In the process of perfecting these IG groups, Jenkins became an expert on this topic, and I highly recommend her material.

Another name synonymous with children in cell ministry is Daphne Kirk. She has dedicated her life to preparing the emerging generation and connecting the generations to minster to each other. She was an early innovator in the cell church movement, traveling extensively with Ralph Neighbour and Bill Beckham in the 1990s. She continues to travel at a demanding pace, teaching churches about the importance of connecting the generations and making sure that children are not neglected in cell church ministry. Two of her many books, *Generational Transformation (*formerly, *Heirs Together)* and *Radical Discipleship* (formerly, *Reconnecting the Generations)*, are a must read for those intending to include children in cell church ministry. She also has developed equipping material for children, which we cover in chapter seven of this book.

York Alliance Church (YAC) in York, Pennsylvania is a shining example of a church's successful inclusion of children in cell ministry. Soon after YAC transitioned to cell church ministry in 1999, they began to emphasize IG cells, in which the children, youth, and adults participated together. Daphne Kirk's visit to the church in 2002 helped transform the way YAC pursued IG ministry. After fifteen years, the IG groups are now a way of life at YAC. New people coming into the church assume that this is the normal way to do church. Many of the current leaders at YAC attended the church as children. They now have twenty active IG groups meeting in homes throughout the area.

The Vine Church in Brazil has been actively developing children in home cell groups since 1999. They now have 10,000 children's cell groups with some 100,000 children participating. The children's home cell groups are very participatory, dynamic, and educational. The Vine views the children as individuals who need to be discipled, knowing that they will soon be adults. When the child reaches the age of thirteen they become part of a youth cell, and later, participants in an adult cell. Testimonies abound of children who were born again in a children's cell group, discipled in the process, and are now preparing to be pastors and church planters.

The Elim Church in San Salvador is also a great example of children's cell ministry. God is developing the next generation through children's cells in San Salvador, a challenging city that has one of the highest rates of homicide in the world. As Elim transforms children, they are making a positive contribution in a country in which gang violence results in thousands of deaths each year. Pastor Vega believes that the high rate of gang involvement (some 30,000 gang members) is because the youth feel marginalized and uninvolved in society at large.

Elim now has about 28,000 children attending their cell groups. Their goal is to reach 100,000 (10% of the city's population) and to make this a reality, they are pouring more and more resources into ministry for children. Transforming children and society is the vision under which Elim develops their children's cells. Elim's ultimate goal is to see their country changed by the gospel of Jesus Christ, starting with the transformed lives of children.[2]

THE AGE OF A CHILD

In this book, I will refer to a child as someone twelve years old or younger. At times I'll distinguish between babies (0-2), toddlers (3-5), and older children (6-12), but for the most part I will just use the word child or children to describe a person from the ages of 0-12 years old. In this book, I will not be discussing youth or youth cells (13 years old and above).

I recognize that the definition of a child is often culturally bound, depending on when a society believes a child is able to take responsibility for his or her actions (e. g., marriage, voting, and so forth) and that the definition has changed over time.

DISCIPLING THE FUTURE GENERATION NOW

The main thrust of this book is to promote and explain how to prioritize and prepare children in both the small group and large group—to make disciples who make other disciples. My goal is to help churches disciple their children and prepare them now for a Christ-centered future. I'll highlight those churches that grasp the significance of starting the discipleship process with children and explain how these churches are ensuring a bright future as some of those same children will fill future leadership roles in the church.

Those cell churches who prepare children for the future have made critical value changes. The leaders believe that God has placed a high priority on children and that this precedence can be seen in Scripture. In the first chapter, therefore, I will explain the biblical base for children's ministry and in the second chapter I'll explore the need for rethinking our strategies based on these biblical truths. Chapter three talks about discipling children in both large and small groups.

Two chapters will explain how IG groups allow children and adults to work in harmony in the discipleship process. I have one chapter on children only cell groups (CO groups), in which the children meet apart from an adult cell.

I will also cover how cell churches equip children and parents. I have one chapter on how to make a step-by-step transition to children in cell ministry. Finally, I will highlight common mistakes in children's ministry and how to avoid them.

Jesus said to his disciples,

> "Who is the greatest in the kingdom of heaven?" He called a little child and had him stand among them. And he said: "I tell you the truth, unless you change and become like little children, you will never enter the kingdom of heaven. Therefore, whoever humbles himself like this child is the greatest in the kingdom of heaven" (Matthew 18:1-4).

What does it mean for the Church today to take this verse seriously? This is a question that has shaped the churches highlighted in this book and their attempt to practice this truth in life and ministry.

Chapter 1
PRIORITIZING THE FUTURE

My brother-in-law, Jeff, excitedly told me about the preparation process behind his future pastorate. He is currently serving as an associate pastor but the plan is for him to replace the lead pastor in a couple years. The lead pastor, in fact, would continue to serve as part of the congregation after Jeff became pastor. Already the church has developed a preaching team, and the lead pastor has been slowly giving away his ministry. One of the key resources for the church's leadership transition was the book, *Next: Pastoral Succession that Works,* by William

Vanderbloemen and Warren Bird. This book highlights successful transitions from one pastor to the next and how to avoid common pitfalls. Vanderbloemen and Bird remind the church that true success is passing the baton to the next generation, rather than abruptly leaving a church without a future leader or failing to leave when it's time for a replacement.

The story of succession and developing future leadership is as old as the Bible itself. Moses developed Joshua before dying and Elijah appointed Elisha before his departure on a chariot of fire. In the New Testament Jesus left the Church in the hands of the disciples, and they followed this pattern in the early Church. The Bible has a lot to say about developing the next generation.

When thinking about passing the baton to the next generation, we often don't start soon enough. The premise of this book, in fact, is that we need to start the leadership development process with children, not waiting until they become adults. Making disciples who make disciples, in other words, is not just for the adults. It involves all ages, including children. But to arrive at this level of thinking, we need to be motivated by God himself and the principles and teaching he has laid out in his Word. And God's Word has a lot to say about children.

Our theology shapes our attitude and our attitude will shape our strategy. Finding the right children's strategy must start with God's Word, the foundation for our lives and ministry. It's not enough to know what to do. We need to know why we are doing what we are doing. Starting with children in the discipleship process—rather than waiting until children become adults—has deep biblical roots.

CHILDREN IN NEW TESTAMENT TIMES

Imagine yourself as a child in one of the hundreds of house churches that developed in the first century Church, not long after Christ's resurrection. Your parents opened their home and even led the house church. You loved the common meal and the remembrance of the death and resurrection of Jesus Christ. You still recall those warm feelings you experienced when hearing about the risen Jesus and how someday you would live forever with him. You gathered with the adults during the singing of the Psalms, the meal, but you also gathered with the other children in the courtyard to learn about God's Word, play games, and sing songs. You noticed that the house servants actively participated and worshipped Jesus just like your parents and the other adults. You even remember the day you first prayed to Jesus and sensed his presence in your life. Jesus, in fact, has become a personal friend and you talk to him every day. Your parents constantly encouraged you to follow Jesus in your attitudes and actions. You are grateful that your parents opened their home and got you involved in the Christian faith at such a young age.

The apostle Paul mentions children in his letters because they were an intimate part of all that took place in those early house church meetings. Many of the children addressed in Paul's letters were probably slave children (some with no knowledge of or contact with their biological parents), and many of the adult slaves no doubt had children.[3] Because the early church was a network of house churches, which occasionally met together in larger celebrations, the children were present at the house meetings as well as the larger gatherings. Osiek, MacDonald, and Tulloch write,

>That children were not merely chance witnesses at early Christian meetings but actually expected to be active listeners to early Christian discourse is made clear by the direct address to them (along with other family groupings) in the New Testament household codes (Col. 3:20; Eph. 6:1).[4]

In New Testament times the extended family lived in the same house, the residents including father, mother, children, and probably one or more married sons with their own wives and children. Workers and slaves were often part of the same household. Since the early Church was organized around this extended family, the need arose for specific teaching on how to behave as the new, transformed family of God. In his letters to the house churches in Colossae and Ephesus, Paul includes instructions (often called the household codes) on how the family-oriented house churches should behave. Paul instructed the children to obey their fathers and mothers.

Fathers, mothers, and children are all exhorted to care for one another and fulfill their roles within the family. John Barclay writes, "The household code assumes the solidarity of a Christian family, and projects an image of the household as the context in which Christian discipleship is given practical expression."[5] Paul gave his instructions to:

- Husbands and wives (Eph. 5:22-33; Col. 3:18-19)
- Parents and children (Eph. 6:1-4; Col. 3:20-21)
- Masters and slaves (Eph. 6:5-9; Col. 3:22-4:1)

Some children were orphaned or saw their parents imprisoned because of their faith. They must have come under the immediate care of the Christian community. For some children the influence of their family was crucial, even if one of the parents was an unbeliever as in Timothy's case. In the Roman world, the role of motherhood was often shared by a variety of people, including nurses, caregivers, and surrogate parents of various kinds. Osiek, MacDonald, and Tulloch write,

> There must have been many cases in which children (especially of lower status) ended up, for all practical purposes, in the care of others, adopted by default; these orphan children may have been habitually fed, occasionally washed, and put to bed by different people. If we add to this the strong possibility that rescuing abandoned children would have been understood as an act of Christian charity . . . we end up with the likelihood that widows often were caring for children who were not their own. The second-century depictions of early Christian groups welcoming ragamuffin children with slaves and women in tow, therefore, was probably not too far off the mark—especially if one observed the "orphans and widows" from an outsider's perspective.[6]

Paul gave his instructions in the plural to clarify that the guidelines are not only directed to the master, wife, children, and servants in one household, but rather toward all members in all households and all house churches—everyone in the entire Church as a whole at that location.

The children saw the faith of their parents not only in the home but also in the local house church community. Therefore, a believer's faith was wisely linked with the behavior of their children. A leader needed to live the Christian life but also successfully transmit that faith to his or her offspring to equip them to successfully lead others (1 Timothy 3:4-5). Children learned through firsthand experience and participation. They were not merely taught ideas, but they perceived how their parents and other house church members lived out the Christian faith.

Children witnessed the powerful prayers and miracles. They were aware of God's goodness through people like Dorcas but also saw God's judgment on Ananias and Sapphira (Acts 5). They were present at the shared meals in the early house churches and saw the believers remembering the Lord's death (1 Cor. 11). They experienced these things first hand and their lives were molded and shaped by what they saw and heard.

JESUS AND THE CHILDREN

Those fortunate enough to be brought up in a Christian home or taken to a Christian church have probably seen multiple pictures of Jesus with a child in his arms. Usually Jesus is smiling and the child is resting securely on his neck or shoulders. Depending on the country, Jesus either has white or dark skin, blond or black hair, and blue or brown eyes.

What Jesus actually looked like is debatable, but we can be certain that he spent a lot of time with children and gave lengthy teachings about a child's closeness to the Father's heart. He even told his disciples that children were the ultimate example of humility and their child-like qualities demonstrated the kingdom of heaven. Jesus taught that God revealed truth to children otherwise hidden from the scholarly and sophisticated (Matthew 11:25). Jesus even set a child in the midst of the disciples and taught them about humility and true greatness (Matt. 18:1-5; Mark 9:33-37; Luke 9:46-48).

At the busiest point of his ministry, Jesus gladly received children and then became angry when his disciples tried to exclude them. His disciples assumed Jesus did not want to be with children. They were wrong. Jesus delighted in children and always gave them special attention and blessings (Matt. 19:13-15; Mark 10:13-16; Luke 18:15-17). Scripture says,

> People were bringing little children to Jesus to have him touch them, but the disciples rebuked them. When Jesus saw this, he was indignant. He said to them, "Let the little children come to me, and do not hinder them, for the kingdom of God belongs to such as these. I tell you the truth, anyone who will not receive the kingdom of God like a little child will never enter it." And he took the children in his arms, put his hands on them and blessed them (Mark 10:13-16).

Jesus so completely identified with children that to welcome a child in his name was the same as welcoming him personally. Yet those who caused a child to turn away from God would face God's anger. The disciples were always obsessing with their own greatness, and Jesus, aware of their inner thoughts, brought a little child before them and said, "Whoever welcomes this child in my name welcomes me, and whoever welcomes me welcomes the one who sent me; for the least among all of you is the greatest" (Luke 9:47-48). Jesus told his disciples that true greatness was becoming like a child.

THE HEBREW CHILD

In the Old Testament, children were a gift from God and part of a larger community. They were connected to parents, grandparents, and cousins—part of an extended family. From an early age, the young Hebrew child was involved in the daily and weekly prayers of his family. He watched the preparation and observance of the Sabbath. He witnessed the sacrificial patterns of his family, and he would have understood that sin carries a death penalty. We can see that these extended families prioritized passing the faith down to the next generation.

The Hebrew family was not an isolated unit. It was part of a larger community, the tribe, which was in turn part of a still larger unit, the chosen people of God. The network of community reached out from the child to the nation at large. Children were educated primarily by their parents who were responsible for instruction in the law, modeling a godly marriage, and also teaching them a trade.

In the book of Deuteronomy, Moses instructs God's people to remember the law and to, "Bind them as a sign on your hand, fix them as an emblem on your forehead, and write them on the doorposts of your house and on your gates" (Deut. 6:8-9). When Jewish fathers prayed, they strapped key verses from the Law to their left hand and forehead, which was a way to provide concrete symbols to the children about the importance of God's Word.

Yet, this was just the beginning. To truly understand God's ways, children needed to see the commandments lived out. Again and again Moses reminds the Israelites that they are to observe, do, and keep God's decrees (Deut. 6:1, 2, 3, 17, 18). Living out God's truth in obedience would make the children different from the non-Jewish people around them.

Moses challenged God's people to pass their faith along to the next generation. He tells them to recite God's laws to their children and talk about them when they are at home, away, lying down, and waking up. Conversation about God and God's laws was not confined to a formal teaching setting. It took place everywhere and at all times. It was supposed to flow freely, spontaneously, and at any time in any place. In this way God became an integral part of the family's life. The child's parents, in other words, lived the faith openly and answered questions as they arose.

Notice Moses does not say, "If your children ask," but "When your children ask" (Deut. 6:20). A God-honoring life of integrity causes children to ask questions, and when they ask, parents need to be ready to listen and learn. Children are naturally full of questions and inquiry. They yearn to know about life, and we need to be ready to answer their questions as those questions arise.

Children comprehend truth through stories. God's people were supposed to recite the miraculous stories of God's deliverance and make sure they were an integral part of the children's lives. It's the story of what God has done in the lives of the Jewish people—their slavery and deliverance. In this story format, the children discovered their powerful, faithful God. Moses instructs the people how to answer their children, "Then you shall say to your children, 'We were Pharaoh's slaves in Egypt, but the LORD brought us out of Egypt with a mighty hand'" (Deut. 6:20-21).

While parents have a significant role to play in the spiritual formation of their children, God does not intend for one man and one woman to carry the full responsibility for their children's spiritual formation. God's plan, seen in Deuteronomy 6, is that the faith community supports the family and together the children receive nurturing. It's best when children see many adults living in loving obedience to God. They can ask questions of people they admire and hear many stories of God at work. It's not only the job of parents to raise and develop children. The people of God are called to participate in developing the next generation.

God's plan for the Israelite children is the same for us today. When we recite God's stories to our children, talk about them in the context of daily life, and remind them of God's faithfulness, they will remember, obey, and follow. Teaching the faith to children strengthens the faith of adults as well. We become stronger as we think of our children and realize they are created in God's image and important to the Heavenly Father.

PASS THE BATON

In a relay race, as soon as the runner receives the baton, he switches it to the other hand so he's ready to pass it to the next runner. Likewise, in the race of life, we're to take baton-passing seriously. Those who pass the baton to the next generation see the potential in children right now.

One seven-year-old boy didn't seem to have a lot of potential because of his Attention Deficit Disorder (ADD). One day his teacher said, "That boy is never going to amount to anything." But a couple of years later the boy was at a public swimming pool in Baltimore, and a man named Bob was also at that pool. Bob saw this kid swimming and went up to his parents saying, "I think your son has potential. Do you mind if I work with him and see if we can pull some of that potential out of him?" They said, "You can, but he's a tough kid to work with." Bob took up the challenge. This boy's name was Michael Phelps, the most decorated Olympian in history. We know his name today because a man named Bob Bowman recognized his raw potential.

Prioritizing the future means getting ready for the next generation by preparing children now for future achievements. The biblical basis for children should lead us to view the potential in children right now. God prioritized children and so should we. Just as New Testament house churches met and networked together, the cell provides a similar environment and an excellent way to develop children. Today's cell church mimics the house church environment as well as the gathering of those house churches on Sunday morning.

Cell-based ministry is a great way to welcome and prepare children both in the large group gathering and the small one. It's a biblically based strategy (Acts 2:42-46; 1 Cor. 14:26) to disciple children at an early age and continue the process as adolescents, youth, and adults.

There are many children right now who can change the course of history in our cities, countries, and nations. God wants to give us a new vision for making disciples of children now in order to equip them to shape the future.

Chapter 2

A NEW VISION FOR CHILDREN

One of the most radical stories in the Bible is about Noah building the ark at the age of 480 and continuing to build it in the face of apathy and ridicule. The Bible tells us that while Noah built the ark, the people lived and acted as if nothing was going to happen. In fact, they thought he was crazy. Scripture tells us that "people were eating and drinking, marrying and giving in marriage, up to the day Noah entered the ark" (Matt. 24:38).

Yet Noah had a God-size vision that controlled everything he did. It was a vision of the future that compelled him to press on, reject the taunts of those who thought he should live a more productive, secular life, and to persist in building the ark until its completion. The writer of Hebrew says, "By faith Noah, when warned about things not yet seen, in holy fear built an ark to save his family. By his faith he condemned the world and became heir of the righteousness that comes by faith" (Heb. 11:7).

Noah is a great example for those who prioritize children's ministry today. His example is a lesson of keeping one's eyes on the future while living in the present, and then practically preparing for what is sure to come.

RIGHT ATTITUDE

The pastors and churches exemplified in this book understood that making disciples of children, spending money on their equipping, and mobilizing the adults to help in the process, would ensure the church a far greater chance of a strong future leadership base. Like Noah, they prepared for a future day.

Yet each one of these pastors can testify that maintaining such a razor sharp focus is not easy. Obstacles and hindrances abound. After all, adults are able to receive didactic teaching, understand the implications of that teaching, and then assume current leadership in the church, whether this means leading a cell group, coaching other leaders, equipping others in the discipleship equipping or even planting a church. Adults can serve as elders in the church and contribute to the bottom line right now.

Because children can't offer the same immediate contribution in the life of the church, they are often neglected or withheld from any leadership training until they grow up or at least turn into youth. Yet, such thinking is flawed because it's short-term thinking and often hinders children from becoming involved in youth ministry.

The churches highlighted in this book looked beyond the current moment and prepared for the future now. They somehow grasped the shortness of time and were able to project that the current children could soon be the future church leaders. They also were enriched in the process and reaped the benefits of working with children. Mary VanderGoot writes,

> Once we take seriously the potential for helping children develop emotional richness, we also discover that children can become our teachers. Children can express in a simple way those emotions that adults, because they are more complex, are less skilled in handling. Children, because of their lack of experience, are not as fixed in unhealthy habits as many adults are, nor are children as crafty as adults in hiding their true feelings and substituting others.[7]

While there are many benefits of working with children, it's also hard work. Children require someone to take them to church, pick them up, protect them, and guide them. It's certainly not easy.

Certain pastors and churches, however, make a commitment to invest in the future, just like investing money in a bank for retirement. Granted, it often seems more logical to spend the money on current necessities. Yet, those who can foresee a future need for retirement, wisely save and reap the benefits of those savings. While the current pastor might not be the recipient, it's the role of the pastor, teacher, apostle, evangelist, and prophet to prepare God's people for works of service so the body of Christ might be built up (Eph. 4:11-12).

RIGHT STRATEGY

Pastor Keison Carrillo couldn't stop talking about children's ministry when I first met him in 2013 in Barquisimeto, Venezuela. He talked excitedly about his cell groups, of which half of them were children's cells. His on-campus educational facilities were immaculate, full of first-class artwork. I talked to the staff involved in children's ministry and was impressed by their creativity and commitment. Pastor Keison told me that it all started when he visited Wales some five years earlier. He wanted to see the land where many of the great revivals took place in the early twentieth century (1904-1905). These revivals kept the churches of Wales filled for many years to come. The revival swept the rest of Britain, Scandinavia, parts of Europe, North America, the mission fields of India and the Orient, Africa and Latin America.

To his amazement, he could only find the grand, empty churches, which at one time were filled. God began to speak to him that unless he prepared the children now, his own church would suffer the same fate. He came back with a new commitment to prioritize children and give them the first place in his ministry. Keison's church, MCM (Misión Cristiana para el Mundo), now has some 250 children's cells and 250 adult cells. Their resources, leadership, and vision are directed to children's ministry. Pastor Keison is radically convinced that children should be formed as disciples who make other disciples.

CLARITY

Keison strongly believes that children are the future now—not just in some future time period when they become old enough to understand better. Keison and his leadership team prioritize time and resources into molding, shaping, and developing children who are practicing Christ's commission in Matthew 28:18-20 when Jesus gave his charge to the Church. Jesus said to the eleven,

> All authority in heaven and on earth has been given to me. Therefore go and make disciples of all nations, baptizing them in the name of the Father and of the Son and of the Holy Spirit, and teaching them to obey everything I have commanded you. And surely I am with you always, to the very end of the age.

Jesus is talking here to his adult disciples, and he is telling them to make more groups of disciples, in the same way that they met in a group with him, interacted with him, participated in his teaching, and spent time with him. Christ's own disciples followed his advice and met house to house in small groups, just like Jesus taught them (Luke 9; Matt. 10). So does Christ's commandment only apply to adults? No. We've already seen that the children were an integral part of the early house churches, and that Jesus pointed the way by prioritizing children in his own ministry. We also reflected on how the Old Testament included the family and the entire faith community in developing children. The theme of making disciples has a direct application to children.

Those churches that see their children as disciples who need to be called and equipped are the best prepared for the future. Those who ignore the children or only see them as static recipients of knowledge pay the price of that inactivity when the children grow older.

INVOLVEMENT

Keison, like other effective pastors working with children, know that children need to interact with the teaching, rather than only listening. Disciples learn best when they can interact with the teaching and practically apply it.

Jesus pointed the way with his own disciples. His teaching was not static, but interactive, practical, and effective. Jesus involved his disciples and even allowed them to fail. Why? Because he realized that mistakes are some of the best teachers.

Those churches who effectively disciple their children also prioritize involvement. They allow the children to get involved in both the cell and celebration. I noticed this same involvement in Keison's church in Baquisimieto. MCM wanted the children to alternatively teach the Sunday lesson, participate on the worship team, and be actively involved in the cell groups.

PREPARATION

Churches, like MCM, who make disciples of children not only minister to them in the cell and celebration but also have a carefully laid out equipping for the children. Daphne Kirk, Lorna Jenkins, and many others have developed complete discipleship equipping for children and a number of cell churches have developed similar equipping for children (chapter 7 is dedicated to this theme).

In my research of churches that effectively disciple children, I heard story after story of current missionaries, pastors, and supervisors who were converted as children through the cell structure and are now diligently serving Christ's body in a full-time capacity. The equipping, in other words, started with the child and continued all the way to Christian ministry.

Effective churches and pastors develop children through a well-defined equipping because they believe that children, just like adults, can hear God, receive from him, and minister to others. The discipleship equipping gives children a huge advantage as they march on through life.

Churches that disciple the future generation now are constantly thinking ahead. They live with the future in view, knowing that the present children will soon be in their early teens and will quickly graduate to the youth ministry. The preparation is not complete unless they graduate to the next stage of their development in youth ministry and beyond. The Vine Church in Brazil, for example, has a special ceremony for those graduating from the children's ministry at the age of thirteen, and they carefully shepherd the graduates into youth cells. Since the children only know the atmosphere of the cell and celebration, they are like fish in water—it's the only environment they have experienced. Children are ready and eager to meet with their peers and continue the process of discipleship.

Some churches, like the First Baptist Church in Campo Grande, Brazil even allow the older children—those eleven and twelve years old—to lead children's cell groups (an adult is always present). This Baptist Church has an eye on the future and wants to give the children an opportunity as soon as possible to practice what they've learned by leading other children.

MOBILIZATION

The best cell churches mobilize the current resources to make sure children are effectively discipled and prepared. The Elim Church, for example, places more time and energy into equipping those sixteen and older to lead children's cells than they do for those adults who will be leading adult and youth cells.

Beyond the general discipleship equipping for all cell leaders, extra, specialized courses are offered to those who will be leading the hundreds of children's cell groups throughout San Salvador.

In her book, *Shouting in the Temple,* Lorna Jenkins explains the transition to children's ministry at FCBC. The church transitioned from ministering to the children only on Sunday morning to ministry on Sunday and weekly IG groups meeting in homes. Yet, to do this, the lead pastor had to affirm that this was a biblical mandate and the future direction of the church.[8] Guided by the pastor's vision and commitment, FCBC grew to be a church of some 10,000 people and 500 cell groups, many which were IG groups.

THINK CHILDREN

Perhaps you're a church plant, starting with a single cell group. Even though you might be in the initial stages, start your church with children in mind—involve them from the very beginning. If you're transitioning the church to the cell model, don't just begin with a pilot group for adults. Plan the first pilot group with children in mind. Allow the first families to invite their children, creating an atmosphere much like the early house churches. Think children and the future will be bright and God-pleasing. Making disciples of those who will be the future generation will provide rich rewards very quickly.

Chapter 3

SIMPLE STRUCTURE FOR THE VISION

Walter Isaacson's book, *Einstein: His Life and Universe*, talks about Einstein's search for simple, clear formulas to understand the universe. His famous mass-energy formula "$E=mc^2$" is amazingly simple. Granted, this formula is still very complex to me, but for those within the scientific community, Einstein's equation was shockingly straightforward and simple. Einstein had a knack for taking existing truths and proven experiments of other scientists and then bringing those concepts together into a simple unified whole.

When Jesus started his ministry, he made it very simple and plain—make disciples. While the Romans and Jewish leaders didn't understand what Jesus was trying to do, he had a clear formula and plan to change the world through making disciples.

His command to his own group of disciples was to continue the process of making disciples throughout the world. They did this in small house churches, which would come together and celebrate whenever possible. They traveled throughout the entire known world implementing this simple discipling process. Even fierce persecution couldn't stamp them out. And the strategy that Jesus promoted is the same one that propels the Church forward today.

Cell church ministry is simple, following the pattern of Jesus Christ. Many people over-complicate cell church ministry, but it only involves four elements which are directed at making disciples:

- Cell
- Celebration
- Equipping
- Coaching

All cell churches highlight these four basic elements. And these four elements apply equally to children as they do adults.

As my good friend Daphne Kirk is fond of saying and writing, "Like adults, like children." She says, "Children have the same needs as adults in many areas of their lives. Most of the problems that are encountered are because their needs are expected to be totally different, and adults then feel that they could never cope with any significant interaction with them."[9]

The focus of this chapter is the large and small group gathering—the celebration and the cell. Both of these elements (or wings) are essential in the discipleship process. A church with these two components is better equipped to make disciples who make disciples than a church that emphasizes one or the other exclusively. Acts 2:46-47 says, "Every day they continued to meet together in the temple courts. They broke bread in their homes and ate together with glad and sincere hearts, praising God and enjoying the favor of all the people. And the Lord added to their number daily those who were being saved."

In Jerusalem, the early Church met in houses to participate in the Lord's supper and fellowship, but then those same house churches gathered together in the temple to hear the teaching of the apostles. We see here both the house church meetings as well as those house churches coming together to hear the apostolic teaching. Children were present in both the small group and large one. Whether meeting together regularly in a larger gathering or only occasionally, the house churches in the New Testament were connected, and this connection has important implications for discipleship.

But what about equipping and coaching? I've dedicated chapter seven to discuss discipleship equipping for children since this element requires a whole chapter.

Coaching is also very important because it ensures that those who are leading the children receive care, encouragement, and development. All cell churches prioritize the coaching of the leaders and those leading children's cells are no exception.

I do not, however, have a chapter dedicated to coaching cell group leaders in this book. The reason is because I have not found the principles of coaching to be sufficiently different for children's cell group leaders than for adult leaders. That is, cell churches coach the leaders of children's cell groups in much the same way that they coach leaders of adult cell groups. When there are coaching distinctions for children's cell groups—like in the Vine Church and First Baptist Church of Campo Grande—I will mention those unique coaching aspects while writing about the particular church. Otherwise, I recommend the books and articles I have already written on the topic of coaching.[10*]

MAKING DISCIPLES IN THE LARGER GATHERING

Many non-cell churches do an excellent job of ministering to children in the larger gathering, and cell churches can learn a lot from them. It's common, for example, for Christian churches to channel money, training, and staff development into children's ministry on Sunday. In fact, part of the Protestant heritage is to gather children during the celebration service to teach and minister to them. The best cell churches also emphasize making disciples in the larger gathering.

Children learn best when the teaching is dynamic and relevant. Lorna Jenkins writes about ministry to children on Sunday,

---

*I've written three books dedicated to coaching and two books which talk about coaching. I recommend these books in the following order: *How to Be a Great Cell Group Coach: Practical Insight for Supporting and Mentoring Cell Group Leaders* (Touch Publications, 2003), *Coach: Empower Others to Effectively Lead a Small Group* (CCS Publishing, 2008), *You Can Coach: How to Help Leaders Build Healthy Churches through Coaching* (CCS Publishing, 2011), *Passion and Persistence: How the Elim Church's Cell Groups Penetrated an Entire City for Jesus* (Touch Publications, 2004), *From Twelve to Three: How to Apply G-12 Principles in Your Church* (CCS Publishing, 2002, 2015). You can also read twenty-seven free articles about coaching at http://www.joelcomiskeygroup.com/articles/coaching/coaching.htm.

The Children's service reflects the adult service, except that it is more children-related. There is fast and upbeat worship, quiet and reflective worship, games, drama, object lessons and memory verses. All these are based around the one central truth, which is presented in the Bible teaching.[11]

TEACHING

One of the key ways to disciple children is to teach them God's Word. Children, like adults, need teaching from God's inerrant Word. Paul's exhortation to Timothy applies to children,

> Preach the word; be prepared in season and out of season; correct, rebuke and encourage—with great patience and careful instruction. For the time will come when men will not put up with sound doctrine. Instead, to suit their own desires, they will gather around them a great number of teachers to say what their itching ears want to hear (2 Tim. 4:2-3).

During the normal adult sermon time, children can have their own Word time as well. Often the children will worship with the adults and then are dismissed from the adult service to gather in classes or altogether, depending on the size of the church.

Some larger cell churches have an entirely separate gathering for children that includes worship, drama, and a general teaching. Then the children are divided into age specific, class-size groups to study God's Word. Trained teachers instruct the children. Those teaching the children should use all possible resources to educate them and keep them interested, such as skits, flannel graphs, dynamic stories, big-letter song books, and anything visually attractive.

Often cell churches will connect the teaching on Sunday with the cell group that takes place during the week. Some more advanced cell churches—like the Vine—synchronize all teaching (sermon, children's ministry on Sunday, and cells). Pastor Marcia, pastor over children's ministry at the Vine, will write the children's material based on the message that her husband, Aluizio, preaches. That same biblical theme is then crafted into a cell lesson for the children, as well as the adults, to be used in their cell groups during the week.[12] Lorna Jenkins writing about her experience at FCBC says,

> Senior Pastor tells the leaders his preaching themes and Bible passages for the coming three months. One of the children's staff divides these themes into weekly topics and assigns a memory verse to each one. At other times, the Children's Pastor sets the central truth, which is to be taught at the Sunday celebration. She then passes these message outlines to teams of volunteer helpers who prepare drama, memory verses and object lesson for each Sunday. [13]

Great teachers get the children involved in the stories through interactive questions. As with any great lesson, preparation makes the difference between a dry, boring lesson and one that has a lasting impact. The goal is to have the children return with a new commitment to serve Jesus. If you're a church plant, you might not have the resources that larger churches are accustomed to. Yet, the goal is the same: envision the children becoming ministers of the gospel—disciples who make disciples—rather than simply recipients of knowledge.

I first understood that Jesus was alive when I was ten years old in a fifth grade Sunday school class. The church I was attending seemed more concerned about rituals, reciting prayers, kneeling, standing, and other postures. It all seemed confusing to my young mind. Yet this particular Sunday School teacher clearly taught that Jesus Christ was alive and wanted to have a personal relationship with each of us. He challenged us with the idea that we could talk to Jesus in the here and now and that Jesus wanted to become a personal friend to those who called on him. I didn't receive Jesus at that moment, but it was certainly an important seed in my own life and one that stands out to this day.

WORSHIP

Teaching God's Word and worshipping with other believers go hand-in-hand. Some call the entire experience "worship." I'm referring here to helping children learn to enter into God's presence, move in the Spirit of God, learn to pray, and hear God's voice. Of course, an important part of this is gathering with other adults and children in a larger gathering.

My own church, for example, includes the children with the adults in the main worship service for the singing. I often see some children in the larger gathering dancing at the side of their parents, swaying to an inner beat and perhaps dreaming of the day that they would be up front as part of the worship team. I rejoice at their spontaneity and freedom in Jesus as the worship songs are played. Then the children go to their children's church where they have additional worship as well as a lesson on their level.

There is something powerful about a larger group gathering that inspires people to seek after God. The larger gathering gives those present the opportunity to be inspired by the awesome majesty of God. Worship in the larger group can help the children become stronger disciples as they get to know God and experience him with others.

I appreciated hearing one worship leader tell the congregation to soak in the presence of God and not to worry about singing the words, posturing in a certain way, or impressing someone nearby. "Your goal," he said, "is to enter God's presence and to love him in a more intimate way." The same applies for children.

VISION CASTING

"We are going to conquer this nation for Jesus, and we're going to start with the children. They are the future. Don't be weary in well-doing; your reward is in heaven." This is the typical rallying cry of pastor Aluizio and Marcia Silva at the Vine Church. They realize that those leading children's cells can become discouraged. They need to be encouraged to press on, and this is where the lead pastor and team play a critical role in the larger gathering. Gabriela, one of the key team leaders at the Vine Church, told me that children's ministry can be discouraging. One reason why they have a yearly rally is to encourage the leaders with God's larger vision for the church and nation. Wise cell church pastors use the preaching, the announcements, testimonies and other means to remind leaders of their eternal rewards, the great things God is doing, and the need for persistence.

The reality is that children's cells require adult help, whether hosting the group, leading the group, or organizing it. So when it comes to casting the cell vision, the lead pastor has an excellent opportunity during the larger gathering to proclaim to all those congregants that formation of disciples is not just for adults. Everyone needs to be involved.

Mario Vega often casts the children's ministry vision on Sunday morning, speaking highly of those who are leading the children as well as plans to open more children's cells throughout El Salvador. Mario's influence adds a new excitement to the church and encourages those who are ministering to the children.

EVANGELISM

Eighty-five percent of conversion experiences occur to people between the ages of four and fourteen. This means that if we are going to make disciples of all nations, we need to start with the conversion of children.

Luis Bush, a well-known missionary strategist, spent the first half of his career promoting the 10/40 Window, the area of the globe between ten degrees and forty degrees north latitude. Bush's thesis is that Christian missionaries need to target their efforts on this area of the world because most of the world's non-Christian population lives in that region. While Bush continues to believe that the 10/40 Window is essential, in September 2009, he announced a new initiative called the "4/14 Window," reaching children between the ages of four and fourteen—the largest and most strategic group of people in the world. His 2009 book is called *The 4–14 Window: Raising Up a New Generation to Transform the World*, and it explains why the evangelism of children should garner both our attention and resources.

The larger gathering is a great place to evangelize and reach the 4/14 Window. I remember during a larger gathering at my childhood church, I heard a speaker talk about asking Jesus into your heart. He showed how this worked via a short film. I was probably ten years old at the time. I don't believe the presenter gave an actual invitation to receive Jesus, but I do remember that I realized that Jesus wanted to have a personal relationship with each person, and that he wanted to live in my heart.

Evangelizing children is not only about conversion but also teaching them to evangelize. Sunday school and discipleship equipping (chapter 7) are great places to do this. Children make friends easily and can naturally invite their friends to Christian activities—and often their parents will come as well. Children, like adults, can exercise their spiritual muscles by evangelizing others, inviting them to both cell and celebration.

DISCIPLESHIP IN THE CELL

At the age of six, Luis was forced to live on the streets in Salvador, Brazil. His father kicked him out of the house and forced him to make it on his own. At times his abusive father would force his brother, sister, and mother to live on the streets as well.

Luis sold peanuts at a nearby gas station and asked for money from people parking their cars at an adjacent restaurant—with the promise to watch their cars while they were eating.

Out of desperation he began to attend a neighborhood children's cell, mainly for the food that was served at the end of the meeting. He felt welcomed. It was like being in a family. He came back week after week and eventually received Jesus.

Jesus transformed his life, giving him hope and purpose. He faithfully attended the children's cell, receiving discipleship, counsel, and support. The spiritual formation he received in that group guided his life and helped him avoid the ravages of the teenage years.

When I encountered Luis, he was a faith missionary at YWAM in Brazil. He and his Indonesian wife now have their own children who they are carefully discipling in the Christian faith. Luis has mastered several languages, is very entrepreneurial (his wife said he could do anything), and has plans to write books.

Cell groups both reach and disciple children. Evangelism and spiritual growth are two key components of cell ministry. But there's more.

WHAT IS A CELL?

A cell (called by a variety of names, such as a life group, heart group, or growth group) is a group of three to fifteen people who meet weekly outside the church building for the purpose of evangelism, community, and spiritual growth with the goal of making disciples who make disciples that results in multiplication.

Notice the goal is to make disciples who make disciples who are bringing glory to Jesus Christ. In Matthew 28:18-20, Jesus is talking to a group of disciples, the same disciples (apart from Judas) he molded and shaped for a three-year period. He had taught them important life lessons as they lived together. Much of the crucial character development came as they worked through conflicts and overcame difficulties with one another. Jesus had called these disciples to join a new community and become part of a new spiritual family.[14] Daphne Kirk writes,

> The children in your cell need discipleship for the same reasons as the adults! Each child is a unique, profoundly precious individual in the eyes of God and their parents. For that individuality to be recognized early in life, they need

someone who knows where they are in their relationship with Jesus and the problems they face.[15]

Jesus felt that the group process was essential in making disciples who make disciples and the same is true with children. The early Church continued the disciple-making process from house to house and children were a vital part of those early house churches. Lawrence Richards writes, "We can visualize the children joining in the times of singing and prayer during the house church meetings. The younger children probably slept, but the older children participated as part of God's extended family."[16] The home is still the best place for children's cells because it is the extension of the family and the natural habitat and environment for growth and development, although some cells might meet in schools, a community center, or even a park.[17]

MORE THAN INFORMATION

The focus of a children's cell group is not just about receiving information, like when a teacher lectures in a classroom. Rather, it's a small group of children—not necessarily the same age—who are growing together, applying the Bible interactively, and reaching out to other children. Lorna Jenkins writes,

> The cell group focuses on friendship, activity, and basic Bible information for kids who don't know the Bible at all. Prayer is also at the heart of them. Kids outside the church are very interested in prayer and how it works.[18]

A children's cell group prioritizes the transformation of those present and the focus is on applying God's Word. When the children open the Bible together, the message is directed at how the children can live out their Christian faith each day.

Children in the cell are encouraged to hear God's voice, pray, and speak out what God is showing them. The Spirit touches lives as each child responds to the Spirit in him or her. Jesus is the Lord of the cell, which is his Church, and he loves to operate and bring about transformation.[19]

The leader is not so much a teacher, as a pastor, role model, and mentor. Everyone joins in the discussion and the youngest children can share an experience, a question, or a prayer which blesses the others. The leader may be an adult, but as the children grow spiritually they can be given more and more responsibility.

Prayer is a vital vehicle for the children to share their needs and encourage one another in their daily lives. They also learn how to pray for the needs of others. Children can be powerful prayer warriors and need to be developed into this vital role.

There are two types of cell groups for children. One is the intergeneration group (IG) and the other is a children only group (CO). The IG group highlights all generations including children, whereas the CO group is led by a team of adults in someone's home during the week. Both are common in cell ministry and the next three chapters will explore these two types of groups in detail.

Chapter 4
INTERGENERATIONAL CELL GROUPS

In 1969, Ralph Neighbour, Jr. formed a non-traditional church in Houston, Texas called "The People Who Care." The church formed home cell groups, where unchurched friends were made to feel welcome. This was a completely different paradigm, but the church had an amazing impact on the city and began to teach others how to start cell groups. Neighbour had no idea that Paul Yonggi Cho was experimenting with the same thing and in the process of becoming the largest church in the history of Christianity.

In 1970, Neighbour visited Cho's church in South Korea. He noticed a children's cell group meeting on Saturday on the steps of a closed building. God spoke to Ralph, showing him that the family of God was being violated by the mentality that the children did not belong in cells. Neighbour returned to Houston and in the early 1970s began developing the idea of IG groups, in which children, youth, and adults mixed and ministered together. While Ralph started the process, it was Lorna Jenkins who perfected it. Lorna earned her doctorate degree at Colombia Bible College where Ralph was a professor. Under Neighbour's mentorship, Jenkins researched children in cell ministry, from both a biblical and practical perspective.

In 1990, Neighbour moved to Singapore to help Laurence Khong develop FCBC, and they invited Lorna Jenkins to implement IG groups. A plethora of material developed on IG groups, equipping children, and connecting the cell with celebration, best captured in Lorna's excellent book, *Shouting in the Temple*.

IG cell groups have a long history in the modern cell church era. They originated with Ralph Neighbour, were fine-tuned by Lorna Jenkins, put into practice in Singapore, and then circulated around the world. Daphne Kirk became a key player in developing children through IG groups and connecting the generations.

WHAT IS AN IG GROUP?

Picture entire families—children, youth, and adults—coming together under the same roof. All those present experience fellowship before starting the meeting and maybe even a light snack. The meeting starts at the agreed upon time and begins with an opening icebreaker. Mary asks, "What is your favorite season of the year and why?" Mary calls on Nancy to start off, knowing her personality and eagerness to share. Everyone is given an opportunity to speak and the excitement builds as people become comfortable with each other.

Then the group begins worship. John, the fifteen year old, plays the guitar and leads the group in common songs with the words printed out. Some of the children sit quietly, while others sing energetically. Nancy, a five year old, can't help herself as she dances to the music. John waits in between songs, giving time for God's Spirit to move, someone to give a word of encouragement, a prophesy, or a prayer for healing.

James and Mary, the leaders, close the worship time in prayer and the kids, normally ages 3-12, are dismissed into a part of the garage which has been converted into an all-purpose room. Beatrice and Mary are taking their turn teaching the lesson to the children, and they make it dynamic, fun, and educational. They also will prepare the children to present a skit to the rest of the adults during the refreshment time at the end of the cell.

In the meantime, the adults apply the lesson, which was based on Pastor Jim's Sunday sermon. Mary facilitates the discussion, asking questions, and avoiding preaching another sermon. After about forty minutes, the six men go to one side of the room to pray about specific needs, while the seven women have their own prayer meeting. At 8:30 p.m. everyone comes together for refreshments and to watch the children's skit. People trickle out about 9 p.m., refreshed by God's Spirit, a deep sense of community, and excitement to serve Jesus.

IG groups are as old as the New Testament house churches because those early groups were intergenerational. They connected the parents, children, and extended family. The Book of Acts speaks of entire households participating in the Christian faith and describes Church life happening in the believers' homes. The Bible refers to the Church as the household of God or the family of God (1 Tim. 3:15; Eph. 2:19; Gal. 6:10). Family language is also used to describe our relationship to one another. The metaphors "God the Father," "Jesus the Son," "children of God," "brothers and sisters in Christ," along with a number of other family terms became a means to communicate a new Christian theology. It also built a foundation of church community and interactions between its members. Paul uses the terms "brothers," "sisters," some 118 times in his letters. Robert Banks writes,

> The comparison of the Christian community with a "family" must be regarded as the most significant metaphorical usage of all. For that reason it has pride of place in this discussion. More than any of the other images utilized by Paul, it reveals the essence of this thinking about community.[20]

Lorna Jenkins defines an IG group this way, "An Intergenerational Cell Group is a cell group that welcomes children as full members. It does not set up any age barriers. Although children may have a separate subgroup during the evening, they belong to the whole cell group, and they can bless and minister to the adults as well as be blessed by the adults. Such cell groups include the children in all their activities: prayer, praise, spiritual growth, and evangelism."[21]

CONNECTING THE GENERATIONS

When York Alliance Church (YAC) in York, Pennsylvania first made the initial transition from a program-based church to a cell church, it made the determination that the cells would be intergenerational.[22]

Pastor Brian Kannel would love to say that it was a wise, well-thought out decision with deep theological grounding. But the reality was that there were a lot of kids, and the church needed to know what to do with them. IG groups answered that question. And in the past fifteen years, they've seen growth and maturity in the children, youth, and adults.

The church began with homogenous cell groups, but they noticed a problem. The young married couples had questions and problems that were very typical for young married couples: How do I decide on a house to buy? When should we start trying to have a family? And so, they asked others in their community. Predictably, they had no good answers. So, they pooled their ignorance and made the best decisions they could.

Meanwhile, as the group of retirees connected with one another, they discovered that while they had a lot of answers, none of them really had any questions. When they talked to one another and compared aches and pains and the current ailment of the day, they found that they didn't have the energy to even ask questions.

The church quickly discovered that IG cells were not simply a strategy to care for children. With an intentionally integrated community, young adults had older men and women speaking wisdom into their lives. Children suddenly had multiple adopted grandparents who loved and cared for them. The energy of young lives was somehow infused into an older generation.

Teens were no longer simply being mentored by a youth sponsor; they were being invested in by an entire family. Single men had a family to eat dinner with; widows had companionship;

empty-nesters had children running through their living rooms again, which they could send back to their homes when they were ready to enjoy their hard-earned peace and quiet.

IG cells connect the best of both worlds. They bring families together to disciple children. They build up both the young and the old. Ideally, an IG cell consists of children, their parents, single adults, young married couples, and senior couples or singles. However, it doesn't have to have all these ages.

Christian parents who have children in an IG cell can continue the discipleship process during the week in their own family. They are not separated from their children; rather, cell life becomes an extension of their family. This helps both parents and children. Yet IG cells also give an opportunity to reach children who don't have Christian parents.

In the IG group, the children are accepted as full members and are encouraged to participate in the life of the cell group. Children have the amazing power to teach, convict, and mold adults. They don't hold back. They share what they feel. Like adults, they can minister to those with needs.

The environment of the IG cell offers the potential for healing of the whole family. Daphne Kirk writes,

> In the intergenerational cell everyone can realize their potential, not in a separate building, not just among their peers, but in the context of Church, in family, in the community that he has created! Here they can move into a relationship with Jesus and His people. Through that relationship they will discover that Jesus really is "the same yesterday, today and forever," and know that they are loved, appreciated and valued.[23]

Daphne Kirk points out that therapy today is offered in the context of the family, recognizing that everyone is important if change is to be effective, and that the interaction of family members is a vital part of that healing.[24]

TOGETHER AND SEPARATE

The children in IG cells meet with the adults in the regular cell format during the icebreaker as well as the worship time.

The children are then dismissed during the lesson time. While the adults interact with God's Word based on the pastor's lesson, the children receive their own personalized cell lesson that is normally prepared by the church. The children meet in a different room of the same house after the icebreaker and the worship.

Some cell churches have a children's ministry pastor or coordinator that oversees the IG groups, provides the material for the IG meetings, and coaches those giving the lesson. This same coordinator is responsible for getting the children's cell guide to the right person. Many smaller churches find their resources in bookstores, the Internet, or by asking gifted parents to prepare the children's cell guides. Some IG groups show a Christian video during the children's time with questions for application.

When the group consistently has four or more children, many groups look for a more permanent team of leaders who feel called to lead the children (more in chapter six). This might be someone from the adult cell group, or from the church.[25] If someone does not feel called to lead the children's cell, the adults can rotate in ministering to the kids. Adults should be encouraged—not forced—to take a turn in leading the children's cell group. Each week a different adult team takes the children and works through the cell guide with them.

The children's lesson time is often called the "Kids' Slot," the time when the children go into a different room after the time of welcoming and worship. The Kids' Slot can be facilitated by members of the small group who are known and who have been in the small group for a period of time. It's always best to have two adults in the Kids' Slot for safety and ethical reasons. During the Kids' Slot, children are encouraged to hear God's Word, interact with one another, and build relationships with each other. Children have the opportunity to interact with different adults and to see God working in their lives. They get to see the "normal Christian life" as lived by the adults in the church.

Children need to have ownership of the small group. They should have the freedom to ask questions, express their opinions, and even give advice. They can be in charge of aspects of the cell meeting, such as prayer, choosing songs, evangelism, and even facilitating parts of the lesson. They should especially be encouraged to serve through the gifts of the Spirit to those in the cell group.

The ages of the children do make a difference. Many IG groups ask babies and toddlers to stay in the adult cell. Often, babies are held by mothers, dads, singles, and "grandparents." The toddlers toddle around during the cell time, usually occupying themselves. Sometimes they fall asleep. At about age three, the children may begin attending the Kids' Slot. Sometimes two to three year olds attend the Kids' Slot, especially if an older brother or sister is also there. But as a general rule, those children younger than three years old should be encouraged to stay with their parents or sleep on a bed or in the parent's arms. They might also play quietly. After a time, children can be trained to accept this and even be taken home asleep.

If those in the Kids' Slot are ages three to six, they'll need more activities, such as singing, games, visual aids or videos. This age group won't benefit from the lesson time in the adult cell. They will need a dynamic, applicable lesson, complete with questions, drama, prayer, and other activities.

One cell reported having six two year olds in the group. They were disruptive in the adult cell and the Kids' Slot. Therefore, this particular group created a toddler group. The cell placed an adult with the six in another room, equipped with praise music and toys. Another cell group had one family with six children under twelve. The baby, Michaela, began coming into the Kids' Slot at about eighteen months. The group found a special role for her. She participated in the art activities and sharing time.

BENEFITS OF IG CELLS

One of the most important benefits of IG cells is that the kids are not compartmentalized into different age groups. The older kids can lead the younger ones and help coordinate places for them to participate. Those in the IG group learn conflict resolution skills about how to interact and make decisions as a team. It's not easy to work with diverse ages and those involved in IG groups have to depend on Jesus to make it work. One IG leader found it was helpful for the children to prepare a dramatized story to present to the adults during the refreshment time. The leader writes,

> The kids get excited about working together to present the story to the adults. Instead of the adults entertaining the kids, it's the other way around. They feel an

important part of the gathering. The kids are not just passively learning about a story—they are interacting with it in a meaningful, experiential way that facilitates learning and life application. The kids feel important and included in the festivities of the house church meeting. It's fun![26]

Children need to know and be known by adults who care about them and invest in them. Relationships can be built through small acts of attentiveness and interest, something as simple as an adult looking deep into a child's eyes and saying, "I'm so glad you're here." In the pressure of doing ministry, we can too easily overlook such small acts of personal care.[27]

GOD WILL DO IT

When the Bowman family first began leading a home group, their biggest concern was the children. They were worried that the children would interrupt and that no one would be able to concentrate. Their fears, however, did not come true.

They learned to relax and allow the Spirit of God to move through the members of the group. They discovered that adults and children learned from each other and everyone grew together. Jessica discovered that ministering to the children in the home group was a fine line between preparing too much (overly formal curriculum) and too little (a wing-and-a prayer). Above all, the Bowmans grew in their relationship with Jesus and the family of God, as adults and children ministered to one another—a lot like primitive house churches in the New Testament.

As you learn to trust God and step out in your IG group, you'll mature in your own faith as well as giving wings to children as they practice their own Christianity. In the midst of the struggles, you and your family will be transformed in unexpected ways.

Chapter 5
THE NUTS AND BOLTS OF INTERGENERATIONAL CELL GROUPS

"I led Jenny to Jesus. She prayed to receive Christ in her heart," Sarah proclaimed. Sarah was only thirteen at the time and had been leading the Kids' Slot for a few months. Jenny was six years old and sincerely wanted to know Jesus. Sarah had spent a lot of time that evening preparing her lesson, and she felt it went well, but she wasn't expecting the joy of leading someone to Jesus.

Sarah was part of an IG group that included adults, teens, and toddlers. She and the kids participated with the adults during the icebreaker and worship, but then the children (ages 3-12) went into the garage for their lesson time. Normally the children would present a skit to the adults during the refreshment time or sometimes the kids would share testimonies. Sarah was grateful that her younger sister, Nicole, helped out.

I remember this story very well because it happened in our own IG group in our church plant in Moreno Valley. The church plant, in fact, began as an IG cell, and we depended heavily on our children to lead worship, help with prayer, and lead the Kids' Slot. We discerned from the beginning that our children would greatly benefit from getting involved in a children's cell from an early age.

Sarah started leading when she was twelve years old, and Nicole, my second born, took Sarah's place and led a group that turned into a youth group that met during the same time as our IG group. Chelsea, my youngest, was always part of an IG group but eventually began to lead a youth life group that met at a separate time. Yet, she learned her leadership skills from within the IG group from her sisters, Nicole and Sarah.

BE IN AGREEMENT

Whenever I do seminars, I like to get as much information as possible about what I should expect and what the church can expect from me. I've learned from experience that it's best to remove the guess work and discover the reality of the situation. The same is true with IG cells and expectations. Churches with IG groups have found that a small group agreement maintains order and helps the group fall back on guidelines when that order breaks down. The IG agreement deals with such issues as how each member will respect host homes, will respond to other members, how the issue of discipline will be addressed, and anything else where people have different standards and boundaries.

The children can discuss various issues independently of the adults, and then adults and children can compare their ideas and reach an agreement. If this is reviewed at regularly stated times (e.g., every two months), then many unnecessary conflicts can be avoided in the small group.

Group Agreement Example

1. It is not good to run inside the house.
2. It is not good to put one's feet on or jump on the furniture.
3. Most people do not like their guest to turn on the TV, stereo, or computer without their permission. Seek consent before playing any musical instruments.
4. It is not polite for a guest to go into the bedrooms or the kitchen unless invited.
5. It is not good to play with objects or toys without the permission of the host. It is embarrassing if something gets broken. Writing on walls and furniture is not allowed.
6. It is polite to help to tidy up any mess before leaving.
7. It is polite to ask the host first before using the bathroom.
8. It is not polite to eat or drink until invited to do so. It is kind to first offer food to someone else before you start eating.
9. Children and adults should thank the hosts for their kindness.

Consistency is a big factor. The main leader of the group needs to maintain the consistent discipline. Kevin Walsh writes,

> In order for effective discipline to take place, there must be consistency between the expectations which parents and teachers hold for the child and the child's ability to achieve those expectations. Too often children are expected to do things which are unrelated to their capabilities.[28]

Daphne Kirk has been counseling churches for years about acceptable and unacceptable behavior in IG groups. She recently blogged about setting down guidelines in IG groups:

- **Distractions:** There needs to be an agreement on how to avoid distractions with the kids. Adults can be encouraged to invite a child to sit with them, so every child has an adult to help engage. If the children are sitting on the floor, each child needs his or her own seat.

- **Participation:** Talk about how to get everyone involved in the cell. Children love icebreakers. It's a good idea to go around the group giving the children the opportunity to answer—just like the adults. Children love to announce the icebreaker, so give them a sense of ownership, asking one of them to announce it. Children should also be engaged in worship. The prayer time should involve the children.

- **Rotation in the Kids' Slot:** There needs to be agreement that alleviates the burden on only one adult. If the same person does the Kids' Slot each week, he or she will miss out on the normal lesson. Each adult should take the Kids' Slot in rotation (in pairs for child protection). If an adult lacks confidence, pair him or her with someone who has more experience.

- **Agreement on outreach:** Often it's a great idea for the children to plan some kind of evangelistic outreach (often called the witness time) in the Kids' Slot or come back and join the adults.[29]

- **Finishing the IG cell:** It's a good idea to be in agreement with the children and adults about how to finish the IG group (e.g., come back together, time to finish group, and so forth).

Having a written agreement about acceptable and unacceptable behavior can not only avoid grief, irritation, and anger, but it can also encourage good behavior such as participation, evangelism, and spiritual growth.

WELCOME

A great way to start an IG group is the icebreaker. Most people are tired when they arrive at the group. They probably don't feel like being spiritual. Some will attend because they know they should be there, not because they feel like attending. Begin on a joyful note. Let them ease into group life.

The best icebreakers guarantee a response. They stir people to talk about hobbies, friends, family background, or personal experiences.

A question is asked to all those present, adults, youth, and children. An icebreaker might be, "What do you like best about Christmas?" or "What is (or was) your favorite subject in school?" Some IG groups who have been around longer might go far deeper in the icebreaker. For example, Holly Allan recounted using the icebreaker, "What are you afraid of?" Some of the responses were:

- I won't pass fourth grade
- I will gain too much weight in my pregnancy
- I will die young like my dad did
- Mommy and daddy will get divorced
- Ben won't get his parole

Jeremy who was in second grade, put his head on his arm and began to cry, saying, 'I'm afraid to go to sleep because I have nightmares." One of the dads in the group came over to Jeremy and put his arm around his shoulders. He held him for a minute, then prayed with him and over him, that God would take away the nightmares. One of the older girls in the group went over to Jeremy and said, "You know, Jeremy, I used to have nightmares, but I prayed to God and he took them away."[30]

Icebreakers can be fun, light, or more profound, depending on the cohesiveness of the group, how long the group has been together, or whether or not the intention is outreach.

Examples of Icebreakers

- Who was your favorite grade school teacher and why?
- When you're stressed or frustrated about something what do you do?
- What's the best thing that happened in your life last year?
- What's your hobby and why do you like it?
- Who was most influential in your own decision to follow Christ? What was that person's relationship to you (friend, parent, teacher, etc.)?
- Ask each one to complete the sentence: "One word to describe me is . . ."
- What's one of the most important pieces of advice someone has given you?
- Describe your week in colors.
- What animal best describes your mood right now?
- How forgiving are you when a friend lets you down?

WORSHIP

Following the icebreaker, the adults and children begin the worship time with the goal of entering God's presence and giving him control of the meeting. Without Christ's presence, the group is no different than a seasonal social gathering or school-related event.

The worship leader doesn't have to play guitar or sing like Darlene Zschech, the famous Hillsong worship leader. I've experienced worship times in IG groups in which the members choked out a joyful noise (with the emphasis on the word noise). Kids don't have the same hang-ups with singing on key and perfect cadence. After all, God looks at the motivation for singing. Some cell groups prefer to play a YouTube video, CD, or DVD, while the members sing along.

Sometimes a child chooses the songs; sometimes a child leads the songs. Sometimes a parent and his or her child will have chosen the songs together. The praise time may last a few minutes or a half an hour, depending upon such factors as the unity within the group, response to the Sunday morning experiences, or the needs of the evening.[31]

I think it's best to flow as much as possible during the entire worship time, rather than stopping and starting to pick the song. I like to intermingle praise and prayer between songs. The leader might pause for praises saying, "Feel free to praise God with a sentence or two, expressing your love for him. Children, we want to hear you as well." God has given children a special sensitivity to respond to him in prayer, hear his voice, and sing to him. This is a time for all of God's people to enjoy his presence and worship as a family.

Don't limit the worship time to only singing songs. The group can experience God's presence through reading Psalms together, praying sentence prayers, or even waiting in silence. Helping children to hear God's voice, pray, worship, and become an active priest of the living God is an important part of the discipleship process.

WORD

Both the adult cell and children's cell normally follow the Sunday sermon or general church teaching. Yet, even if the church provides the lesson, it's essential that each small group leader examine the lesson and apply it to the needs in the group.

The leader of the Kids' Slot for that particular week will read the Bible story, give a short lesson, ask questions based on Scripture, and might even ask the children to dramatize or act out the Bible lesson. The children might recreate a Bible lesson they learned on Sunday and then present it to the adults during the refreshment time.

Keep the teaching on the child's level. Sometimes teachers love big words that only the initiated can understand. Speak simply, clearly, and use a lot of stories to illustrate what you're talking about. Children crave words that are understandable. Andre Kole, one of the top illusionists in the world, said, "The hardest people in all the world to fool with your tricks are children."[32] That's because children aren't as complex as adults in trying to figure something out. They just see life for what it is.

After explaining the biblical story or text, the facilitator than asks questions to stimulate understanding and application. Daphne Kirk promotes using questions like:

- How did that make you feel?
- What would our group be like if we all lived that Scripture?
- What changes do we need to make in our lives if we are going to live that Scripture?
- What do you think God is saying to us right now?[33]

Without fail, God speaks to the group through his Word, and people recognize their needs.

WITNESS

The last part of the cell, the witness or works time, helps the group to focus on others. There is no "one way" to do this. The main thought that should guide this time is outreach, which might vary on a weekly basis:

- Praying for non-Christians to invite
- Preparing cards to send to a missionary
- Helping a hurting family with food and clothing
- Praying for family members who don't know Jesus
- Planning for a future multiplication

Specific prayer requests naturally flow from the lesson time. Children can pray for one another, for their friends, for their family members, and for those who they plan on inviting to the next IG group.

COMING BACK TOGETHER

Many cell groups have a refreshment time at the very end in which children can share what they learned in the Kids' Slot. Doing a skit for the adults about what the children learned is a great way for children to reinforce the biblical truths from the lesson. It also gives the parents an opportunity to ask questions and interact. Sharing with the adults might be as simple as the leader of the Kids' Slot asking someone in the group to share what he or she has learned. After one child shares, others will probably want to add what they learned.

An IG Group Gathering

Welcome
Children and adults together
- Welcome (Cell leader welcomes everybody, including the children by name)
- Icebreaker (Children participate)
- Reporting, sharing

Worship
- Worship, mingled with praise, prayer, and listening to God. Scripture reading is an important form of worship.

Word
Kids' Slot
- Edification: Discussing the Bible story or Scripture verse; Learn a memory verse
- Activity: Praying for unbelieving friends and family, world, and so forth; Plan for service to others

Witness/Works
- Works (Sharing the vision, planning events, evangelism, multiplication date, and so forth)
- Prayer
- Children return to adult group
- Food and blessing (Children and adults all share the fellowship and relationship building at the end of the meeting)

YORK ALLIANCE CHURCH

When Jacob Shuey was in fourth grade, he was part of an IG group at YAC. Now, eighteen years later, at age twenty-eight, he leads an IG group. "It's amazing to hear the wisdom of a sixty year old when you're only a teenager," he told me. "That's what intergenerational groups are all about," he said. When his family moved to York, PA, his entire family became involved in an IG group. His dad and three younger brothers continue to be part of life groups and have stayed faithful to Jesus Christ.

Jacob and his wife Amanda have been leading an IG group for about five years. The group has twelve adults and five children. The willing adults take turns in leading the Kids' Slot. "We like to have two men lead the Kids' Slot together or two females. One of the reasons is for spiritual bonding—to get to know each other."

VALUE CHANGES

The leadership at YAC has concluded that it's better for people from different walks of life to learn from one another and to mentor each other. Pastor Brian Kannel knows this is contrary to human nature. "The desire among people is to communicate with their own age group," he told me. "Yet it's essential that they don't simply pool ignorance. Among very young people, no one has the experience to say, 'you should be doing this.'"

From the beginning, Brian realized that the YAC membership had to personally "buy-in," or adopt the intergenerational philosophy. "In some cultures," Brian said, "the lead pastor practically dictates what he wants everyone to do. At YAC, our people don't respond to a heavy-handed approach."

It hasn't been an easy road, but the church now believes it made the right decision to transition to the IG model of cell ministry. Kids are not an add-on to the group or the responsibility of a select group of people, but a vital part of each group. Every group member speaks truth into the lives of children—and listens to the Holy Spirit through them, as they speak into the lives of the adults.

Although the church passed through times of resistance and diverse obstacles, it held firm to its IG group decision because it was based on deep values. From the beginning they believed this was the biblical model that would help mature the different generations within the church. "It's still work," Brian told me, "but we increasingly recognize the eternal biblical values associated with IG ministry." The church has become the family of God in a very real way.

A WAY OF LIFE

Fast-forward a decade at YAC and children who had once been in Kids' Slot are now becoming teens who are deeply engaged in the life of the group and the IG community.

Several teens have gone through cell group intern training and have taken responsibility for the leadership of their groups. They are no longer just participants but now want to ensure the future success of their groups. In the church as a whole, the barriers that were once there are largely gone. "And frankly," Brian said, "the reason there is no resistance is because this is all they know." And even more exciting is the booming group of young adults at the church. Far from having left the church, as many of the statistics predict they would have, the young adults are deeply connected to the church and even leading the church forward. Twenty-five percent of the groups are being led by people in their twenties, many who have grown up in the IG cell model.

Of course, there are still issues, as there always will be. However, the decision to have IG cells is one that the church has never regretted. Now it's a way of life, and people are actually promoting the vision to others.

FOCUSING ON THE HEART

At one point YAC had a pastor who would prepare the Kids' Slot messages. Yet, they felt that this became a duplication of the educational model. Now they have a three-pronged approach. The first prong is Sunday, which is more curriculum based, the normal teaching of children.

The second one is the application focus in the cell groups. The Kids' Slot normally includes Bible application, worship, prayer, and games. The leader will talk to the children about their pursuit of Jesus. "The focus is on the heart," Brian said. We want to make sure that each child knows Jesus and is growing in a personal relationship with Jesus." The goal is for the Kids' Slot leader to be authentic, process faith with the children, and build relationships with the children.

The church does background checks on those who lead the children and the newer leaders are always teamed up with the more experienced ones. Most groups rotate adults to teach the children, but they don't force adults to take a turn. It's voluntary. They always have two people leading the Kids' Slot—either two males or two females. "We see it as a bonding time between the teachers as they minister to the children," Brian explained. There's also plenty of material available in the church for the lessons, since YAC has been doing IG cells for fifteen years.

The third prong is Christian service. YAC has a Wednesday night children's outreach. The focus is on those families with children who want to participate in outreach projects. About twelve children attend, along with adult volunteers.

FLEXIBILITY

Even though YAC prioritizes IG groups, they don't ask all teens to be in the groups with their parents. Teens might join another IG group. Every leader has the freedom to develop the IG connection that works best for that particular group. Pastor Brian's group, for example, has several very young toddlers while others have older children. YAC celebrates the variety among the IG groups, while carefully coaching the leaders of each group so as to make sure that the leaders are properly equipped and cared for.

Pastor Brian admits that they are still a work in progress. Yet more and more they are discovering the many benefits of IG ministry and are excited about the future.

LITTLE FALLS CHRISTIAN CENTRE

In 1988 Harold Weitsz took over a church of 385 people near Johannesburg, South Africa. By 1994 the church had grown to approximately active members, but there was a great need for a proper care system aside from the traditional method of pastoring. While on a ministry visit near Cape Town, he was introduced to Ralph Neighbour's book, *Where Do We Go from Here*, which changed the direction of his ministry. Weitsz joined a group of South African pastors who went to Singapore to hear Neighbour present an advanced cell training course and to experience FCBC, the cell church where Neighbour and Lorna Jenkins were both ministering at the time.

Today, Little Falls Christian Centre (LFCC) is a fully transitioned cell church, with some 3,000 people, 300 cell groups, and dozens of church plants. The church leads seminars throughout the world and is an inspiring model to many. Their website says,

> With the implementation of home groups we saw the care system redirected from the Pastoral Team to the home cells. The cells became the care teams and the Pastoral Team was released to take care of all training and serious problems that could not be handled by cell leaders. The church literally started adding members daily.[34]

One thing that is less known about LFCC is their commitment to children in cell ministry and specifically their IG cell groups. At LFCC children minister to adults and adults in turn minister to children in the cell. Children are included in everything the cell does: icebreakers, prayer, praise and worship, ministry, evangelism, prayer walks, and so forth. Children grow up to practice an active Christian life in the cell environment.

The Bible lesson for the children takes place in sub-groups called Kids' Slots, while the adult part of the cell continues their lesson. Normally the children who join such a cell are the children of parents in that cell, but the cell is not limited to children of those parents.

LFCC believes that IG cells fulfill most completely the biblical model for the spiritual nurture and growth of children:

- The children are seeing their parents involved in Christian life (role models).
- The children see other models of Christian life (other people in the cell).
- The children can be actively involved in worship and service in the cells.
- The families in the cell learn from and encourage each other.
- The single parent families find a secure extended family in Christ.
- New families that join the church enter the IG groups together as a family unit.

The IG groups at LFCC encourage each adult in the cell to be involved in ministering to the children each week. As with most IG groups, different adults take turns at leading the Kids' Slot, but it's not compulsory. This gives each adult in the cell the opportunity to know the children and minister to them. The children in the cell gain by getting to know all the members and respecting them.

The parents are supplied material through the children's ministry from the local congregation. Yet, it's the cell group leader who is responsible to make sure that the Kids' Slot will take place.

The hosts have the right to determine the "house rules" for behavior of children in their home. The entire cell group has a group agreement about how the group should behave and children are part of that agreement. Any cell member may remind a child of the agreement they made as a group.

Children from 4-12 years old participate in the Kids' Slot. Babies and toddlers sit with their parents, and the parents are asked to supervise their own children. After age twelve, the child is encouraged to attend youth cells, but some teens prefer to stay with the parents in an IG group, and this is fine. Many prefer a youth cell group, so there are different options.

Children, whose parents are not in the cell group, can still attend the group, but they need to be sponsored by one of the Christian families within the adult cell. Although the adults are the main ones who lead the Kids' Slot, older children can be given responsibility in Kids' Slot as junior leaders.

IG groups function best when everyone knows what to expect and each group follows agreed upon guidelines. Yet, it's not just the children who need to follow particular rules, adults also need to follow clear guidelines. These guidelines are very similar to the IG rules we discussed earlier. One unique area at LFCC is the guidelines for the adults:

- Take responsibility for one's own children.
- Be patient with the children even when they are difficult to handle.
- Talk to the children, help them, and try to understand them.
- Support the house rules set by the host family.
- Talk to any child who is breaking the rules.
- Get the child's permission when talking about him to the whole group.
- Tell one's own children when delegating authority to another adult.
- Involve the children in the group activity.
- Do not allow the meeting to run too late. This gives parents the opportunity to take their children home.

The IG groups at LFCC have been very effective over the long-haul, partly because the goal is to share the gospel. To do this, each member is encouraged to talk to friends and neighbors about Jesus with the goal of inviting them to the IG group. The church not only mobilizes those outside the church but also those within. Pastor Weitsz, for example, regularly preaches about cell values and the importance of preparing children in cell ministry from an early age. The church also holds meetings with the parents to encourage them to bring their children and get involved.

LFCC multiplies IG cells in the same way they multiply their other cells. Each IG leader is encouraged to invite the group members to attend the LFCC equipping with the goal of starting new groups. The IG leader, along with the supervisor over the cell, guides the process of group multiplication by allowing adult members to participate in different parts of the IG group, including leading the lesson.

ROBERT LAY AND IG CELL GROUPS

Since 1998, Robert Lay and his ministry, Ministerio Igreja em Células, has trained over sixteen thousand pastors and leaders in cell church principles and values. After many years of consistently teaching the values and principles, there are now large, healthy cell churches from many, many denominations in Brazil. In addition to teaching the modules, Lay's ministry has added two national conferences, five regional conferences, and translated over seventy cell church books into Portuguese.

Lay's ministry has also developed curriculum for IG groups. Lay emphasizes the importance of the parents' responsibility for the Christian education of their children. He believes that the cell church strategy is helping churches change their attitude toward children's ministry. Lay says, "The task is not easy. The church is swimming up river and having a hard time changing today's culture."

The biggest struggle, according to Lay, is getting parents involved in the Christian education of their own children. To change this reality, Robert Lay and his team offer seminars for parents and for teachers (facilitators). "Sadly," Lay said, "most churches are not willing to invest in this area. They have not awakened yet to the importance of investing in the best future leadership of the church, our children."

Robert Lay's material has three pillars:

- The church on Sunday
- The cell
- The home

Lay's ministry has developed seven years of curriculum for children that connects Sunday, the cell, and family home devotional material taught by the parents. For each month, there is a manual to be used in the church, one for the cell, and another given to the parents to teach the children at home.

Connecting one biblical theme to all three spheres of life really drives home the biblical application to the child. The child also benefits from the teaching on Sunday, life experience in the cell during the week, and then receiving interaction with the parents at home. They have manuals for all age groups, from nursery children to age twelve.

The Sunday material is geared around age specific children's classes, and the materials offer a wide variety of suggestions for interaction and dynamic teaching. All age groups on Sunday have the same Bible story, from which one main principle is taken. That same principle is reinforced in the cell and in the home, during the same week.

Even though there are many mega cell churches in Brazil, most cell churches are small and have only one Sunday celebration service. During the celebration, children leave the room during the sermon, and divide in classes, according to their age groups. Those churches that are larger can divide into more age specific classes and still use the material with more specificity to a particular age group.

The cell portion of Lay's material is geared toward the IG group in which parents participate in the Kids' Slot, each taking a turn to lead the lesson. Lay thinks that children should be mixed within the IG groups and not separated from parents. He believes that the New Testament description of the house church meetings show that children were involved with the adults and all of them were part of the family of God.

For the home part of the material, the manual covers the same theme but offers practical suggestions for parents to have their family devotional time. Lay teaches that parents have the primary responsibility in developing their children, so they've designed material to help guide them in the process. Parents are empowered when they can remind the children of what they learned on Sunday and during the IG group. The children's prior knowledge allows for deeper interaction between parents and children.

Lay believes that developing a children's ministry requires flexibility, as well as persistence. He emphasized his personal beatitude, "Blessed are the flexible ones, because they will not be broken." "Our materials allow adaptations and variations. The most important aspect, though, is parents being responsible and involved in the developing of their children."

There are now hundreds of churches using these materials. Lay said, "We have great testimonies of families being positively affected and transformed. We keep an open channel with the churches that use our materials, and we hear stories of transformation. We have churches from all denominations using our materials."[35]

FIRST BAPTIST IN CAMPO GRANDE, BRAZIL

Located in the western state of Mato Grosso do Sul (bordering Paraguay and Bolivia), Campo Grande is a bustling city of about one million people. Near the city center is the campus of First Baptist Campo Grande (FBCG), led by Senior Pastor Gilson Breder. As lead pastor for the past twenty-four years, Breder has both vision and passion to reach the lost through multiplying cell groups, planting churches, and sending out missionaries. Beginning with a single cell group of leaders, the church now fields 300 groups and sixty of these groups are IG groups.

One unique aspect of the IG groups at FBCG is the involvement of the children in missions and outreach. The children in each IG group are encouraged to adopt a missionary and to pray regularly for that missionary. The children creatively send gifts, offerings, and cards to the missionaries. I noticed a missionary fervor in the church, and it started with the children. Missions is not just something that takes place over there.

The children are also encouraged to reach out to their friends and neighbors. Neto, for example, is only six years old, but he spoke to all of his friends about Jesus, and they became curious about his faith. They wanted to know about Jesus, his church, and how they could get involved. As the friends of Neto began to talk to their parents about Jesus, the parents talked to Neto's parents saying, "What is your son talking about?" Neto's parents told them about Jesus and invited them to the cell group. Some came to the cell, the celebration, and were even baptized.

Isabella is ten years old. Jesus placed a passion in her life to serve him, and she wanted to complete the training, be baptized, and eventually lead her own cell group. The problem was that her parents weren't Christians. Yet, they saw the change in her life and wanted the best for her. Isabella started taking the Tuesday equipping, which would also prepare her for baptism. The parents got involved with the church through the change of their daughter. As it says in Scripture, "A little child will lead them" (Isa. 11:6).

Like in the case of Neto and Isabella, God is using IG cells not only to transform children but also to reach out to those who don't know Jesus. The harvest is plentiful and the laborers are few, and God is using the children in churches like FBCG to reap the harvest.

Pastor Gilson's wife, Vashti, directs the children's cell ministry. The church uses Robert Lay's material, and their IG groups are similar to other churches, in that adults in the IG cells take turns leading the Kids' Slot.

Pastor Aldezir, another staff pastor, offers training to the parents who will be leading the Kids' Slot each week. Although pastor Aldezir provides the training, the cell leader is in charge of making sure that each parent guides the children through the material. They like to have two adults present to lead the children's part of the cell group. A normal IG cell group at FBCG lasts no more than two hours, which includes the fellowship time. Newborns and those under two are asked to stay with the parents within the adult cell.

I was told that the greatest struggle was to get the adults in the cell to step up to the plate and actually take a turn in leading the Kids' Slot.[36] Sometimes young children help out as well. I talked to Rachel, for example, who is leading the Kids' Slot in her parents' IG cell. She is ten years old. She gathers the kids in a separate room during the Word time and ministers to the younger children.

CREATIVE STRUCTURES

IG groups have been part of the cell landscape for quite some time. They go back as far as the New Testament, but in modern times were recreated by Ralph Neighbour and fine-tuned by people like Lorna Jenkins and Daphne Kirk. Model cell churches throughout the world are implementing IG groups with great effectiveness. But IG groups are not the only way to make disciples of children through cell ministry. God has opened new creative ministry to children in the cell world and one of those innovative methods is children only (CO) cell groups, the topic we'll explore in the next chapter.

Chapter 6
CHILDREN ONLY CELL GROUPS

In 2011, Elim celebrated twenty-five years of cell ministry. During the stadium celebration—where only cell leaders were able to attend—Marisol's father received a plaque for being one of the leaders who have provided faithful and uninterrupted cell leadership for twenty-five years.[37]

Marisol was just four years old when her parents converted through an Elim cell, and it wasn't long afterwards that they were leading their own cell group in their home. Marisol at a young age became accustomed to the cell environment, and she can't even remember a time when a cell was not meeting in her home. Marisol grew to love the cell environment, growing increasingly aware that this is the way to do New Testament church.

As time passed, Marisol began leading prayers, and then the singing in her parents' home cell group. Eventually she was baptized in water in the church.

At sixteen she began working as a leader of a CO cell and has not stopped leading one for twelve years. Today Marisol is twenty-nine and still remains dedicated to teaching children in the cell and in the celebration. She has mentored many girls who are now adults and even leading their own CO groups.

CHILDREN ONLY GROUPS VERSUS IG GROUPS

CO groups meet weekly outside the church building (normally in homes) just like the IG groups, but they meet separately from the adult groups. In other words, the children don't mix with the adults for the icebreaker and worship but have their own icebreaker, worship, lesson, and vision casting time.

The children who attend IG groups normally come with their parents to the group, but this is often not the case with CO cell groups. In fact, the Elim Church will often target densely populated neighborhoods with the goal of starting CO groups. Those attending come from the packed housing sectors in that particular neighborhood.

This was also true in Cusco, Peru where the Vine Church has started 400 CO groups, with many of them meeting completely apart from an existing adult cell group. With CO cell groups, neighborhoods full of children can be targeted without the need for a fully functioning adult cell to make it happen.

Granted, many CO groups do meet at the same house as the adult group and often at the same time, although this is not always the case. In other words, there is more flexibility when using CO groups.

Another key distinction is leadership. In the IG group, leadership is shared. Adults rotate to teach the Kids' Slot. In the CO groups, there are dedicated leaders who are considered the leader(s) of that particular cell group. CO cell groups are treated as normal cell groups within the church. Having a dedicated children's leader also allows for more flexibility in where and when the group will meet.

Like the adult leaders, all those who lead CO cell groups must go through the church-wide equipping, just like the leaders of youth and adult cells. Like all leaders, those leading CO cells are thoroughly coached and cared for by the church's leadership team.

The order for the CO group is similar to a normal IG group:

- Welcome
- Worship
- Word
- Witness

The difference lies in the welcome and worship times because the focus in on the children, rather than children and adults, like the IG groups. Because the icebreaker is only directed to the children, the leader can focus on children related themes. He or she might decide to connect the theme of the lesson with the icebreaker.

If the lesson is on forgiveness, for example, based on how Joseph forgave his brothers, the leader might ask the children to act out the story of Joseph being rejected from his brothers in Genesis 37:12ff. The leader might ask a child to play the role of Joseph going to his brothers to give them food. Other children can play the parts of the brothers. A couple can act out the parts of Reuben and Judah who tried to save Joseph.

The leader can then ask the children about a time when they were not understood or when someone treated them roughly when they were trying to help out. The responses might lead to praying for one another.

Since the worship time in a CO group is not with the adults, it can be more geared toward the children. Worshipping, sharing testimonies, asking for prayer might be part of the worship experience in a CO group. Some ideas to get children involved in prayer and worship include:

- Ask the children to share a time when God answered prayer. Praise God together for those answered prayers.
- Have each child say a short prayer for the person beside him or her, first asking the children what they would like prayer for. The leader should also ask for personal prayer as well.
- Ask the children to spend time quietly, listening to what Jesus would want to show them. Then have each child share what Jesus showed him or her.
- Ask the children to pick favorite worship songs and then ask one or more children to lead those songs

The Word and witness time in a CO cell are the same as the IG groups. If the CO cell group is meeting at the same time and place as the adult cell group, the children can share what they learned with the adults during the refreshment time.

ELIM SAN SALVADOR

Several years ago I wrote a book about Elim called *Passion and Persistence: How the Elim Church's Cell Groups Penetrated an Entire City for Jesus*. I noted three words to describe this church: Passion. Persistence. Penetration. Elim is all about passion and persistence to penetrate the city through multiplying cell groups. The Elim Church has a great cell system, but they have more than just the system. They have a contagious passion that makes the discipleship process work. This passion manifests itself in the commitment of the people to serve Christ and others—including the children.

A cell leader at Elim must be sold out to Jesus Christ first and foremost. Second, the leader must practice the vision of penetrating a city for Jesus through making disciples who make disciples. "Multiplication is a triumph because it means reaching more people for Jesus Christ," Pastor Mario Vega said. With 110,000 people in 9,000 weekly cell groups, the mother church in San Salvador is a shining example of effective cell ministry.

Many have described the Elim Church as an army conquering enemy territory. I would simply add that it's a passionate army, rather than a stiff, cold militia. The people at Elim are passionate for Jesus Christ and their love for Jesus encourages them to expect great things from God and to attempt great things for God. Many other words and phrases describe Elim: servanthood, evangelism, and leadership, but none of them describe Elim's heartbeat like passion.

RESCUING THE CHILDREN

Elim is also passionate and persistent about saving and discipling children before they fall into the clutches of gang activity. Juan, a four year old, was living in a very poor, crime infested neighborhood in San Salvador when he first started attending an Elim cell group. The cell leader asked Juan what he wanted to be when he grew up, and Juan responded, "I want to be a gang member." But things have changed. After several months of experiencing love and gospel values, Juan now says he wants to be a firefighter when he grows up.[38]

Elim is trying to change the culture of El Salvador by actively involving children in cells, transforming their lives with the gospel message, and then preparing them for cell leadership. Elim's CO groups are not only evangelizing children, but they are also a place where children feel family warmth and care—something they have not known or experienced in their own homes. They also gain a purpose for their lives, based on eternal, kingdom values.

Elim will often target crime infested areas of the city with the hope of rescuing children before they are recruited in gangs. Jenny, for example, was sent to open a children's cell in a very poor house in the center of San Salvador. An older lady and her eight-year-old grandson, Leonel, lived in a small, messy house. The neighborhood children packed the house to overflowing each week. Jenny recalls the messiness of the home and lack of space as the children crammed in each corner to hear God's Word, memorize Scripture, worship God, and pray together. Leonel's rooster would often peck at Jenny as she gave the lesson. Despite the difficulties, Jenny pressed on for the sake of the children.

Jenny noted that Leonel was very depressed and sometimes spoke about not wanting to live anymore. Jenny asked if something was wrong, but Leonel always avoided talking about his problems. Over time, and after talking to the grandmother, Jenny pieced together Leonel's history. Leonel's mother was impregnated at the age of thirteen by a gang member and turned Leonel over to the grandmother. Leonel's father had to flee the country, and Leonel never heard from him. He had only seen a photo of him. To survive, Leonel and his grandmother tried selling roasted bananas on the city streets.

The good news was that Leonel received Jesus in the children's cell and began the process of discipleship week after week. He memorized the verses and faithfully attended each meeting. Leonel's mood changed dramatically, although he would sometimes become discouraged because of his living conditions. Many of the neighbors around Leonel were gang members, and Jenny knew he was vulnerable. She gave Leonel special attention, praying fervently that he would stay strong. She asked him to help her in the cell, which made him feel important and needed.

Leonel did make it through those difficult times. He's now seventeen and testifies of God's grace in his life. "Before I didn't care about even living, but now I have a new purpose in life," Leonel says. "Jesus is my priority now, and he's helped me to avoid the mistakes of those around me." Leonel now attends an Elim youth cell as well as the weekly celebration services. He is currently finishing high school and his dream is to study mechanical engineering in college. He's polite, respectful, and a trophy of God's grace—someone who was rescued by an Elim cell group in the dark, broken city of San Salvador.

EVANGELISM AND EDIFICATION

Elim's CO groups are led by those sixteen years old or older. They sprout up all over the city, wherever Elim can find a willing host. The cells are often held in the same house as the adult cell, but the children meet in a different room and are separated from start to finish, although the children might gather with the adults during the refreshment time. Many CO groups meet several hours before the adult cell group on Saturday night.

Normally, one member of the adult cell leadership team will sense a calling to lead the CO group, go through the required training, and then become the leader of the CO group.

The Elim CO cells function a lot like the adult cells. Like the adult groups, participation is promoted and the emphasis is on both evangelism and edification. There is an initial icebreaker followed by a time of sharing God's current work in the lives of those present. A confession time and praying for one another follows. Worship, sharing, and Bible memory verses are key aspects of each group. After this, the adult facilitator leads an interactive lesson. The leader tries to dramatize the lesson and will get the kids involved to make the teaching more dynamic. He or she reminds the children of the need to reach out and to share the gospel with their friends, family, and neighbors. Refreshments follow.

LEADERSHIP PREPARATION

Pastor Mario is passionate about discipling the next generation and transforming the street gangs into harvest workers for Jesus, but he also knows he needs equipped and competent leaders to get the job done. It might seem paradoxical, but Elim's training for children's cell leaders is more extensive than the training for adult cell leaders.

That is, all cell leaders (adult, youth, or children) must go through the normal six month equipping, which is embodied in the book, *The Equipping Route*. The booklet contains twenty-six lessons that cover basic doctrine, how to pray, baptism, temptation, and how to lead a cell group. Unless there are character issues, the person who completes the six month equipping is able to lead a youth or adult cell group or at least form part of a leadership team.

However, to lead a CO cell group, an additional eight months of training is required. So it takes fourteen months to lead a CO group but only six months to lead a normal adult cell group. The additional courses for those leading CO groups include:

- Biblical theology of childhood
- Childhood education
- Children and adolescents with traumas and addictions
- Child protection policy
- How to teach children (pedagogy)
- Dynamic teaching methods
- Identifying child abuse

Because many of the children in the CO groups live in gang-infested neighborhoods of El Salvador, cell leaders are prepared to spot and deal with childhood addictions, trauma, and child abuse. Leaders are trained to make sure the cell activity and lessons are dynamic, fun, and fast-moving, especially since many of the children have lower levels of education and short attention spans.

Cell leaders also know that one of their main goals is to create a sense of love, acceptance, and belonging in the cell group—something that the children lack in their own homes. In this way, the CO cells at Elim are creating a sense of family, love, camaraderie, and a clear alternative from the insidious gangs that are common place throughout San Salvador.

EXAMPLE OF AN ELIM CHILDREN'S CELL LESSON

Welcome and Initial Prayer
Worship through Song (10 Minutes)
The Widow's Offering

Icrebreakers (10 Minutes)

- Why is it important to give God offerings?
- Can only rich people give offerings?
- Is God concerned about the amount of offering?

Lecture: Mark 12:41-44

Searching the Scripture (10 Minutes)

- Did the rich give a lot in their offering? (v. 41)
- What did Jesus say about the widow's offering? (v. 43)
- What did Jesus say about the offerings of the rich? (v. 44)

Teaching (10 Minutes)

1. **The offering of the rich.** As Jesus stood by the box where people were placing their offering, he noticed how the rich were giving large amounts of

money. Most likely the people watching were admiring the great amounts of money that the rich were giving. However, God is not impressed by outward appearance. He sees what's going on in the heart. It's more important to God what's happening inside us than the outward appearance.

2. **The offering of the widow.** Jesus saw a poor widow who gave just a few cents. Even though she had so little to give, she actually gave more than all the rich people. The widow gave sacrificially from the little she had to live on, while the rich gave their extra money that didn't require much sacrifice.
3. **What God sees.** Jesus explained to his disciples that the rich only gave from their abundance but that the widow gave all that she had. She gave the money that she used to buy food to live on. She gave from her heart, but the rich only gave what they could afford to give.

Summary: What goes on in our heart is most important to God. God isn't as concerned about what we do as why we do it. Great amounts of money don't impress God; what impresses God is the motivation of our heart. Think about what your heart looks like to God. To be pleasing to God, a person must receive Jesus Christ as Savior and Lord. God knows if a person has done this sincerely or just to make a good impression. Receive Jesus with all sincerity.

Application (5 Minutes)
- Are there times you do good things but for the wrong reasons?
- When do you care more about how you look to others than how your heart looks to God?
- What are things you do to impress people? How can you turn your heart so you desire God's best for you instead?
- How can you be generous and give to God sacrificially instead of merely giving God what you don't need?

Invitation to Receive Jesus
Memorization: Mark 12:44 (10 Minutes)
Offering and Final Prayer (5 Minutes)

CO CELLS AT FIRST BAPTIST CAMPO GRANDE

We met this creative, dynamic church in the last chapter and noted that their sixty IG groups focused on missions and outreach in a city of about one million inhabitants.

FBCG also allows adolescents to lead CO cells, as long as an adult is present. The adult is ultimately responsible, but the adult doesn't actually lead these CO cell groups—the older children, or adolescents lead them.

Tuesday night leadership equipping is geared toward older children (11-12) and some thirteen year olds, like Gabriel, who is dedicated to lead a CO cell group (more on equipping at FBCG in chapter 7).

FBCG has also developed a top-notch coaching structure for their children's ministry. They have several people on fulltime staff who coach the supervisors who in turn coach those who are leading CO cell groups. Those coaching the leaders—both pastors and supervisors—do a lot of one-on-one coaching, visiting the cell groups, and also gathering the leaders into a larger coaching gathering on Tuesday night. After the equipping time on Tuesday night, the staff, supervisors, and leaders meet together to talk about the progress of the CO groups. The coaches help the young leaders to facilitate the next lesson, practice effective small group dynamics, and grow as disciples of Jesus Christ.

Gabriel, for example, has already gone through the equipping, but he still attends Tuesday meeting to receive help on his cell lesson, general encouragement, and specific areas of need. Although the church gives him the lesson and goes over the main points, Gabriel realizes he is ultimately responsible for the lesson and the CO group in general. "I make adjustments to the cell lesson to fit the needs of my own group," Gabriel told me. "I want to make sure I'm ministering to their needs."

Gabriel has multiplied his CO group three times since he has been in charge, although the cell itself has multiplied seven times. An adult sits in the cell with him to provide accountability and help the parents who send their children to feel more secure.

Gabriel plays guitar, so he leads the group in worship. "But I don't want to do everything," he told me. "I try to get others to lead the icebreaker, the prayer, and other activities in the group." Gabriel's cell meets weekly in the same house, but it is not connected to another cell group. Rather, parents from FBCG have opened their home for Gabriel's group. FBCG prefers to have a more or less "permanent location," so those attending will know where to go each week. At age thirteen, Gabriel is the oldest in the group, but not by much. The other children in attendance are between five and twelve.

I asked Gabriel if he wanted to be a pastor, and he told me he wasn't sure. His parents quickly chimed in, "We want Gabriel to know God's calling for him, whether it means being a doctor, teacher, dentist, or pastor."

Laura, a twelve year old, is another adolescent cell leader at FBCG who leads a CO group. Her parents are Christians and were brought up in the church. She is very shy, but she has been an integral part of a group for quite some time. As she participated in all aspects of her group, she realized that she could lead one. Her parents encouraged her to go to the Tuesday equipping.

As Laura invited children to the CO group, the group began to grow. She brought four friends to the group, and the group multiplied. One of those friends, Laureen, received Jesus, and became a strong follower of Jesus. Laura taught Laureen about the importance of the devotional life, how to maintain a godly attitude, and how to share with others. Now both Laura and Laureen go to the equipping on Tuesday night, although Laureen's parents are not yet believers. The parents allow Laureen to attend the CO group and Tuesday equipping because they've seen such a dramatic change in her life. They like what they see and don't want to hinder God's work.

MCM IN BAQUISIMIETO, VENEZUELA

Baquisimieto, Venezuela is the home of an exciting cell church called MCM (Misión Cristiana para el Mundo), which we met in an earlier chapter. Apostles Keison and Belkys Carrillo are the founders and lead pastors. Keison was part of the revolution that brought Chavez into power, and he has three bullets in his body to prove it. Since Keison and Belkys started the church in 2002, they have grown to 5,000 people and 500 cells. The main pillars of the church are:

- Church growth
- Helping the poor
- Children's ministry

Of the 500 cells, 250 are CO cells. Their adult cells are a mixture of couples, singles, and youth, while their children's cells are the CO variety.

Keison caught the vision for children's cells when visiting Wales and seeing all the empty buildings. "This is the land of revival," he thought, "and there are now only empty buildings.

If we fail to develop the children, we ourselves will have empty buildings." God showed him to focus on the children in everything they do.

I was amazed at the original art paintings that decorated the children's classrooms. Those who visit the Sunday celebration are treated to visual stories of the gospel painted on the walls. The entire church seemed geared around equipping the children of Venezuela.

All leaders—adults, youth, and adolescents—must complete the discipleship equipping track which includes:

- Encounter retreat
- Basic Christian doctrine
- How to lead an effective cell group

One conviction that pastor Keison emphasizes is for children to actually minister to other children. On Sunday they often will have children take part of the lesson or lead the worship. They like to talk about children preaching on Sunday to other children. The conviction of children in ministry spills over to the CO groups, which are often led by those between the ages of 10-14 years old.

I interviewed several adolescents who told me how they finished the equipping and were now taking full responsibility to visit, prepare the lesson, and pastor their CO group. As I talked to three children (11-12) who were leading CO groups, I was amazed at their zeal for Jesus. They were excited about serving him, practicing the spiritual disciplines, visiting the children in their cells, and even preaching the gospel in their neighborhood. I felt like I was talking to young adults or at the very least, mature youth leaders.

The CO groups meet in the homes of adults to offer security and protection. They always have an adult present to ensure against abuse or other problems. The children's ministry staff prepare the cell material, which is connected to the Sunday lesson. MCM does an excellent job of connecting the Sunday school theme with the material for the CO groups. Their children's cell ministry has become so fruitful that they now have conferences on how to develop and grow CO group ministry in other churches.

THE VINE CHURCH

The Vine Church started in 1999 with a gathering of sixty believers in the Brazilian city of Goiania, located in the western center of Brazil. Aluizio da Silva and Marcelo Almeida are the co-founders of this sprawling, worldwide movement.

Aluizio oversees the work in Brazil and Marcelo supervises the Vine work overseas (Europe, Africa, and North/South America). The church has grown to become a network of 800 churches with 45,000 adult believers in the mother church in Goiania. The mother church has some 5,000 cells, which are a mix of adult cells, youth cells, and children's cells. One exciting, unique aspect of this church is their emphasis and commitment to children's cell ministry.[39]

GROWTH OF THE CHILDREN'S CELLS

In 1999, Marcia Silva, Aluizio's wife, prayed and fasted for God's purpose and design for her own ministry in the church. She felt like God was calling her to minister to the children and that God wanted her to do it through the cell groups.

As she looked around, she noticed there were very few models of children's cells to follow. She received a prophecy that same year, telling her to follow God's direction, and that he would give her new direction, a new path to follow. She opened her first CO group and watched God prosper the ministry. By the year 2000 there were forty-two CO groups and 190 kids in the cells. The church had already been transitioning to the cell model, so CO cells became an intimate part of the mix from the beginning.

God gave her an ever-growing conviction that children were members of the body of Christ and were often neglected, and God confirmed his direction by helping her multiply the number of CO cells to the current 10,000 with 100,000 children attending these cell groups worldwide.[40] In the mother church alone, there are some 2,000 CO groups with 20,000 people attending them.

RADICAL KIDS

They call their children's network "Radical Kids." Marcia and her team have dug deep to understand the values behind children's cell ministry and the three most important are:

1. **God is a God of generations.** He is not just the God of Abraham, but of Isaac, Jacob, and all those who would later believe in Jesus. He is concerned that each generation wins the next generation. God has called the Church to pass the baton of faith safely to the next generation, which means winning the children of the current generation who will eventually win their own generation.
2. **Children are part of the body of Christ.** If they are part of the body of Christ, they must not be neglected or forgotten. The church must not give them less attention because they are small and helpless. The only requirement to be part

of the body of Christ is to believe and be born again, and children are an example of simple, sincere faith.

3. **Developing disciples who will win the next generation begins with children.** The discipleship process begins as children. The church must think far into the future and start right away to prepare disciples who make disciples. This means concentrating on the children.

The Vine believes that children are best prepared to become disciples in the home environment, just like adults. They also realize that they will never reach the multitude by requiring the children to come to the church building. Rather, the Vine takes their CO groups to the neighborhoods.

The Vine Church has a growing number of testimonies of those who were born again in a CO cell, trained through the children's ministry, and now serving fulltime in ministry as pastors and missionaries. John Paul Alves is an example. He accepted Jesus when he was eleven years old at a CO group. His parents had been taking him to the CO group since he was four years old.

He then went to an Encounter retreat for children and God touched him in a powerful way. He was healed of his bronchitis. When he turned twelve he was baptized in water and began the Spiritual Maturity Course. He became a leader of a youth cell group, which multiplied three times. He then began to coach four cell leaders.

In the process, God placed a calling in John's heart to become a pastor. He received various prophetic confirmations, and in 2011 he entered the church's equipping for future ministers. Through the equipping, God broadened his vision and after two years he became a pastor in the church overseeing a network of youth cell groups.

John is now twenty-three and one of the many pastors and missionaries who were discipled through the children's ministry and now are in pastoral leadership. The Vine is intent on preparing the next generation of church leaders by starting with the children.

FEMALE CELL LEADERS

The wives of pastors in Vine Churches are mobilized to help out in the children's ministry. The church prefers that women lead CO groups, although they do have some male CO leaders as well. They are not opposed to men leading the CO cell groups, but they have found that female leaders are more readily accepted in Brazilian society, and parents feel more comfortable when women are leading the groups. In their culture, people often jump to conclusions about men working with children, assuming that they are more likely to abuse them.

COACHING NETWORKS

Those leading the CO cells are normally the wives of the adult cell leaders. The local church pastor's wife is the pastor responsible for the network of CO cells and leaders, so she develops a coaching network for all of those who are leading the CO groups. Depending on the size of the church, the pastor's wife might have additional fulltime staff under her or just volunteer coaches-supervisors of cell leaders. The wife of the pastor, therefore, is responsible to develop the network of CO cell leaders and to make sure they are properly coached.

The coaching of the CO leaders takes place on a weekly basis. The Vine uses the name disciplers for those who are coaching the women cell leaders. In the weekly coaching meetings (discipleship gatherings), the coach will pray with the leader, ask questions about the leader's life, and go over any problems in the cell. These discipleship meetings ensure that the leader is not running on empty but has a place to receive encouragement and counsel. Once per month, the disciplers will go over the cell reports to ensure the quality of the groups.

Apart from the weekly discipleship-coaching time, the children's cell leaders also receive fellowship at the cell group. The wife of the adult cell leader normally leads the CO group, so she fellowships with the other adults during the refreshment time.

WHAT A CO CELL LOOKS LIKE

The CO groups meet in homes and normally at the same home where an adult cell is meeting, but in a different room in the house. Parents can bring their children to the same house where they are already meeting, which helps breed confidence. In fact, normally, the CO groups are birthed from the adult cell groups. At one point they started to open CO groups apart from the adult groups, but they discovered that it just didn't work as well, since many children depend on adults to bring them to the cell gathering.

Unlike IG groups, the children do not meet with the adults for the icebreaker and worship. They are immediately gathered into their own cell group. The very young children (0-3) stay with their parents in the adult group. Those who are 4-12 years old attend the CO group. I was told that there is often 15-20 children present in the CO cells.

The CO groups are very dynamic, full of worship and interaction. The Vine has an entire department who prepares the materials for the leaders and provides handouts for each leader. The lesson theme is based on the church's general Sunday teaching but adapted for the children.

The children are also taught to reach out, pray for the sick, and live the Christian life in front of their friends and family. In one cell, the children were asked to pray for a pregnant mother who was in danger of losing her baby. The children knew this mother and insisted on visiting the mother and laying hands on her. As they did, the mother and unborn baby were immediately healed.

The children and adults usually come together at the end of the cell for food and fellowship. Because the CO cell leader is often the wife of the adult cell leader, she has contact with everyone in the group.

EQUIPPING THE CO LEADERS

The Vine Church asks CO leaders to be at least sixteen years old. Although the majority of children's workers are adult females, quite a few young people from the youth ministry participate as leaders in the CO cells.

The Vine only has one equipping for all those leading cell groups, whether adult cells, youth cells, or CO cells. The children's ministry was very careful from the beginning not to create a different structure for those wanting to be children's leaders.

The first step is an Encounter retreat. In the mother church in Goiania there is an Encounter every weekend. The Encounter starts on a Friday and ends on Sunday. People are saved, set free from sin, healed, and filled with the Spirit. On Sunday, people testify of how God has changed their lives. Then the person goes through the rest of the equipping. They call it the Winner's Path. The steps are:

1. Encounter retreat
2. Living Water course
3. Baptism
4. Consolidation course
5. Spiritual Maturity course
6. Leaders Training course

All those in the church are encouraged to take the entire equipping, and finishing the equipping is a requirement for leadership. The Vine has a mission to develop an army of leaders who can change the world, starting with the children. Each children's cell leader is encouraged to develop a team of leaders, so that the process of multiplication can continue.

SUNDAY KIDS

In the Sunday celebration service, all the children celebrate together through worship, drama and general teaching. The children see and hear the story interacted in drama. Then they have age specific teaching in the classrooms. The teaching on Sunday is also applied in the CO group. The children experience the same teaching as the adults but on their own level.

Once per year they have a huge rally to celebrate the ministry of children. What is the purpose of the rally? Encouragement and vision. Because there are Vine Churches all over Brazil, many of the churches are small. When the leaders from smaller churches see all that God is doing at the large rally, they are encouraged to press on with children's ministry. Some 10,000 leaders come to this event each year. The women see themselves as part of a larger vision.

The Vine's example is spreading to many churches in Brazil. As they grow and see transformed lives, many are wanting the Vine to share what they are doing and how they are doing it.

CHANGING OLD PARADIGMS

One of the main difficulties the Vine confronts is the mentality that ministry to children is not as exciting as other ministries. Gabriella, one of the team leaders who oversees the children's cell ministry throughout Brazil, said, "The old mentality is that wives don't want to work with children. There is no reward in this. It's not something exciting. We at the Vine are breaking this mentality." Many wives are now realizing that the children are the future, and that they need to be discipled prior to their becoming adults. The Vine churches are aware that they are influencing many other churches in children's ministry. They are helping churches throughout the world prioritize children in the discipleship process.

Another oft-heard phrase was, "We just don't have enough leaders." While leadership development is always an issue, the Vine discovered that the harvest workers are coming from the harvest. As the children grow, complete the equipping, and become youth, many are becoming leaders of CO groups. They are also finding that more women are catching the vision to disciple children.

THE VINE IN CUSCO, PERU

In the 1990s Cusco, Peru was known as the graveyard of missions and churches. Missionary agencies poured lots of money into Cusco, paying the salaries of national pastors for years. But when the foreign funds dried up, the pastors moved on, and the churches died.

The Vine is different. It is completely indigenous, has 900 cell groups (500 family cells and 400 CO cells), a staff of eleven pastors, and fifty church plants. The Vine in Peru is intimately connected to the Vine church in Brazil. As I talked to the pastors on staff, I realized that each one of them moved along the same progression:

- Converted in the cell
- Cell member
- Part of the cell leadership team
- Cell leader
- Multiplication leader
- Supervisor
- Network leader
- Part of the pastoral team

No one, in other words, is asked to come on staff who wasn't naturally developed in the cell system. I asked Luis Alberto, the lead pastor, "So those who are fruitful in multiplying cells become part of your pastoral staff?" He replied, "Fruitfulness is one of the measures. However, we also want to ensure that the leader is godly, called to be a pastor, and has the right attitude."

I was impressed that most of the pastors were twenty-five to thirty years old and completely willing to stay in the mother church or plant a Vine Church. It became clear that God is using the cell system at the Vine to change the Cusco "cemetery" culture into an explosion of harvest workers.

Their adults cells are comprised mainly of married couples, although it's possible to have a single woman or man leading a mixed cell. They also have mixed youth cells, led by either a male or female. The CO cell groups, however, are the fastest growing segment of groups in the church.

The CO cells are led by adult females—and specifically those who are over the age of sixteen. Jenny, the pastor's wife is the pastor over the CO leaders. She has two additional overseers who help her lead the children's ministry. The overseers are wives of pastors on staff.

Only the women lead the CO cells, and normally the wives are the ones mobilized to lead this important ministry. They believe that women have more influence over CO cells because male leadership is perceived as having a problem of potential abuse. After school CO cells are much more acceptable when the parents know that females will be leading them.[41] They insist that all CO groups have two leaders.

The CO groups meet weekly all over the city in different neighborhoods. If they can't find a home to host the cell, they will meet in parks or other available space. Those attending the cells are from the ages of 3-12. Each group will determine when they will meet during the week. The children are encouraged to invite their friends and neighbors. When the cell gets too large, they multiply.

The groups follow the children's material from the Vine Church in Goiania, Brazil. There is one general theme for the month, which is used both in cell and celebration. The cell groups start with an icebreaker, then worship, a lesson time based on the pastor's message, outreach time, and announcements—just like the mother church in Brazil. The theme for the group is expounded in the Sunday worship service, where children are treated to theatre, dance, and teaching. They encourage Sunday Kids' to be very interactive. That same theme is then applied in the cell group. They have the help from the children's pastor to make this happen. Thus, there is harmony of the theme of celebration and cell.

All leaders of CO groups must go through the equipping track, just like the adults. To take the equipping, the person must be in a cell group and recommended by the leader. They follow the exact same equipping that the mother church uses in Goiania, Brazil.

THE VINE IN ENGLAND

Giles Stevens, lead pastor and founder of the Vine Church in England, is British born and has work extensively in Asia, Europe, and South America. As the son of a British army officer, he was raised in Hong Kong, Russia and Germany and various UK locations. In 2005 he and his wife Silvia relocated to Brazil, where Silvia was born and raised. As a young girl, Silvia had a vision of the Union Jack and bringing revival to the UK.

Both Giles and Silvia worked as network pastors in the Vine Church in Goiania, Brazil for a number of years. In 2009 Giles and Silvia returned to the UK with a vision to raise up a new generation of dynamic leaders through a network of cell churches. The church now has nineteen cell groups, six of which are CO groups.

The CO cell groups run very similar to the CO cell groups of Brazilian churches. They meet either after school between 4-6 p.m., or alongside the adult cell groups between 7-9pm. The only difference is that in European culture, children tend to sleep earlier during weekdays, so a lot of the CO groups meet on Fridays, rather than Wednesdays. The children's leaders are mostly females in their twenties and thirties who dedicate themselves to equipping the next generation.

Like all Vine Churches, the children begin their equipping process in an Encounter retreat (more about equipping in next chapter). In England they have their Kid's Encounters every six months from Friday evening to Sunday afternoon at a local retreat center. Slowly and surely, the Vine is establishing a culture in the church where children and children's ministry are prioritized (Matt. 18:3-5).

HARVEST WORKERS

The CO cell groups allow for added flexibility when reaching children. A new group can start in an unreached neighborhood, like many groups at Elim, MCM, or the Vine Church.

We've seen in this chapter how Christ is developing his Church to reach children through multiplying cell groups. But Jesus is also thinking of future harvest workers. While on earth, Jesus saw the people as sheep without a shepherd and said, "The harvest is plentiful but the workers are few. Ask the Lord of the harvest, therefore, to send out workers into his harvest field" (Matt. 9:37-38). Jesus told his disciples to pray for new harvest workers to reap the harvest. But where will these new harvest workers come from?

Effective cell churches realize that a significant number of the next generation of harvest workers will come from those children who are currently in the cell groups. These churches are actively involved in equipping the children and preparing them for future ministry, the topic of the next chapter.

Chapter 7
EQUIPPING THE CHILDREN

"When you spoke about discipleship equipping, it all made sense," one pastor told me. He sat through all of my PowerPoint presentations about the definition of a cell, cell church history, cell church principles, and even how to make the transition. The equipping, however, was the vital ingredient that made everything clear.

I had been coaching this pastor for several months, but his traditional view of church education hindered him from understanding how to make disciples who make disciples through specific equipping. This pastor, like so many others, was accustomed to promoting general Christian education on

Sunday. It suddenly dawned on him that there was a major difference between education and equipping.

Education never ends. Equipping or training, on the other hand, touches specific skills and lasts a limited time. Neil F. McBride, a Christian educator who has written extensively about small groups, says,

> Education is an expanding activity; starting with where a person is at, it provides concepts and information for developing broader perspectives and the foundations for making future analysis and decisions. On the other hand, training is a narrowing activity; given whatever a person's present abilities are, it attempts to provide specific skills and the necessary understanding to apply those skills. The focus is on accomplishing a specific task or job.[42]

McBride's insight about equipping being a narrowing activity versus the lifetime process of education touches the nerve of discipleship equipping. The best equipping prepares the people to understand the gospel message, basic Christian doctrine, and how to lead a cell group. The process is called by a variety of names: equipping track, training track, school of leaders, or the equipping route. I prefer to use the term discipleship equipping because it clarifies the reason for the equipping: to make disciples who make disciples.

There's one major problem. Most cell churches provide discipleship equipping for adults only. Children have to wait.

This is an understandable error. After all, equipped adults make better parents and can lead future cell groups. But is this pattern short sighted? I think so. The reality is that adults are already on their way out. They've lived a good portion of their lives. And many potential adult leaders are already busy and don't have the time, energy, or desire to take the equipping or lead a cell group. Children, on the other hand, are moldable, willing, and have an entire life ahead of them.

DISCIPLESHIP EQUIPPING FOR CHILDREN

Discipleship equipping for children follows the same basic principles as equipping for adults:

- One equipping. It is best to have one church-wide equipping that everyone is expected to go through (although adapted for various age levels).
- Many ways to teach the one equipping. Some churches teach the equipping during the Sunday school hour; others primarily teach the equipping 30 minutes before the cell group, asking the leaders to take members through it. Others use retreat settings. Some use a combination of methods. In other words, there is a wide variety of ways to teach the equipping, and churches should be creative in helping people complete it.[43]

The cell lesson is different from the discipleship equipping. People often assume the discipleship equipping is the same thing as the cell lesson and that the cell facilitator teaches the discipleship equipping during the cell group. However, the lesson and the equipping are two distinct entities:

- The cell lesson: This is what the cell facilitator uses during the cell meeting. The lesson is normally based on the church's weekly teaching and is comprised of questions that focus on application that leads to transformation.
- The discipleship equipping: This uses a series of manuals with instruction in basic doctrine, evangelism, spiritual disciplines, and small group dynamics. It is taught separately from

the cell meeting and normally takes a certain amount of time to complete.

The purpose of the cell lesson is to apply God's Word to daily living and to evangelize non-Christians. The equipping, on the other hand, explains how to pray, read the Bible, have a devotional time, receive freedom from besetting sin, and other aspects of the Christian life, which are essential for discipleship. Although the equipping for children needs to be adapted for children, the basic components are the same.

DAPHNE KIRK'S EQUIPPING

Daphne Kirk has dedicated her life to making sure that one generation equips the next one and that the process of discipleship continues until Jesus comes. She travels extensively around the world with her son Andrew and daughter Daniella, promoting the need to develop the next generation—before it's too late. Daphne Kirk's discipleship equipping for children is called, *Living with Jesus*.[44] The equipping was written for parents to disciple their children, though the discipler is called a "special friend," so this could be another adult. The themes of the equipping include:

- Welcome to God's family, introducing children to the body of Christ
- Talking and listening, introducing children to hearing the voice of God
- Staying protected, introducing children to spiritual warfare
- What do we choose, introducing children to make kingdom choices
- Having faith, introducing children to a life of faith
- Strongholds, introducing children to strongholds, the soul, and freedom

- Love for me and love for others, introducing children to the unconditional love of Jesus
- Special times and gifts, introducing children to baptism, communion, and the Holy Spirit

The equipping books promote conversation and interaction, rather than one-way teaching. The goal is for one child to meet with one parent or adult once a week. The books are not devotionals but encourage parent and child interaction.

The purpose is to disciple the adult as well as the child. For example, many adults struggle with hearing the voice of God, so during the topic on hearing God's voice, it can be a time for the parent to reflect on his or her relationship with Jesus. In each book, there is a section for the adult as well as the child to complete. One book covers approximately two months of instruction.

Daphne recommends that her books not be given to children to take home to their parents. Rather, they should be given to the adults during an introductory session of the equipping. The parents or adults, rather than the children, should be held accountable.

Along with her equipping, Daphne has prepared cell lesson material that corresponds with each equipping theme. The equipping and the lessons can be used independently of each other.

There are many ways to use Daphne's equipping material. Daphne recommends a variety of training methods such as retreats, experiential teaching in a small setting, and one-on-one discipleship.

She recognizes that some children from Christian homes might know a lot while other children might be hearing about Jesus for the first time. For this reason, she recommends that a church analyze the needs of each child and implement the equipping to satisfy the needs.

EQUIPPING AT FIRST BAPTIST CAMPO GRANDE

At FBCG, the equipping is taught every Tuesday night year round. In May 2015, there were fifty children under the age of twelve who were taking the equipping. The equipping topics include:

- Bible doctrine
- Spiritual growth
- Baptism
- Leadership principles
- Evangelism
- Missions
- How to lead a cell group
- Multiplication
- Supervision (coaching)

Part of the equipping prepares children to be baptized and lead a cell group. After the equipping, those children who are leading children's cell groups are coached on how to facilitate the lesson, icebreaker, prayer, and vision casting time. They are also coached personally to determine if they have personal needs, prayer requests, or problems in the group.

Isabella, for example, came from a non-Christian background. She received Jesus in an IG group and then asked her parents if she could come to the Tuesday night equipping in the church. Her non-Christian parents saw the positive changes in

Isabella's life and decided to take her to the Tuesday equipping. They were so impressed with what they saw that they continued to bring Isabella to both the cell group and the equipping.

Now those same parents have received Jesus, have been baptized, and are faithfully attending the church. Isabella also completed the equipping, was baptized, and eventually began to lead a CO group. Isabella is a serious Christian and is always asking what she should do with the lesson each week. She is not content with just hearing from others about the lesson. Rather, she tweaks it to fit her own cell group. She might even challenge her coaches on Tuesday night by saying, "I don't think this will be good for my cell group. I don't think I'll use this part."

JOEL COMISKEY'S EQUIPPING

Most churches have an adult equipping which can also be adapted for children. This is true with my own equipping. I've written a five book series that takes a person from conversion all the way to facilitating a small group, or being part of a team. Each book contains eight lessons that are designed for interaction and practical application. The child being equipped should be involved in a cell group to get the most out of the teaching.

The first book is called *Live*. The first chapter, "Finding God," explains how to have a personal relationship with Jesus. The subsequent chapters equip the believer to live a fruitful Christian life by explaining prayer, Scripture, Christian fellowship, receiving a new identity in Christ, obeying Christ's commands, and administrating God's resources. A child can both find Christ and grow in him by studying this book.

The next book is *Encounter,* which guides the child to receive freedom from sinful bondages. Jesus said, "You will know the truth, and the truth will set you free" (John 8:32). All people, including children, need this freedom. The book begins by teaching how forgiveness is the only way to overcome hurt and resentment. It then instructs the child on how to forgive and receive forgiveness. The book also shows the child how to receive the fullness of the Holy Spirit and then to walk in the Spirit. The book can be used individually or in a retreat setting.

The third book, *Grow,* helps the child understand how to hear God's voice, meditate on God's Word, and practice the presence of God through worship. *Grow* explains how to have a daily quiet time in order to know Christ intimately and grow to maturity. *Grow* outlines how to seek God in the quiet time and explains the amazing benefits of experiencing God on a daily basis.

The fourth book, *Share,* describes how the gospel is the best news on the face of this earth. Children need to learn to boldly proclaim the good news of Jesus Christ to classmates, neighbors, and family. This book also instructs the cell group on how to plan outreaches, pray for those who don't know Jesus, and invite children to special cell activities.

The fifth book, *Lead,* prepares the child to eventually lead a cell group, explaining all the parts of a cell and what is required for cell leadership. It explains how to facilitate a cell and grow in the process. This book highlights key small group dynamics that will give the leader confidence in facilitating others.[45]

Churches like City Harvest in Australia have effectively used my equipping with younger children. Crystal Dickson, a leader at City Harvest, has used my equipping with those between the ages of 10-15 years old. She wrote the following to our ministry:

> This discipleship series has been working really well, and I'm nearly finished teaching the 5-book series. The girls that I am discipling just love the material. It's written in easy to understand language, and they like the life stories and examples that relate to each lesson topic. One of the girls in my group was baptized a few weeks ago, because the Holy Spirit spoke to her as she was doing the lesson about baptism and communion from Book 1.

Churches might start by using a prepared equipping like my own with the goal of making their own material. It is critical, however, that children are also invited to participate in the equipping and that it's not for adults only.

LORNA JENKIN'S EQUIPPING

Lorna Jenkins developed an extensive discipleship equipping for children while working at FCBC. She believes that every church should have a discipleship equipping. She writes,

> How can we bring children to Christ and then not teach them what the Christian life is all about and how to draw on the power of God in their own distressing lives? Many children are facing big problems of life, big fears, big situations and big temptations at a time when they have few spiritual tools to handle them. Even the parents are not always aware of the shadows their children are facing—especially in this world of cyberspace.[46]

Jenkins's equipping starts with young children with the hope that they will complete the equipping by the time they are twelve years old, although there is flexibility.[47] Writing about her pioneer experience of equipping the children, she writes, "Preparing children through the equipping was one of the most effective things we did and the children loved it." She continues,

> If we are serious about leading our children into spiritual maturity and ministry, we need a systematic way of doing it. We cannot rely on a "hit or miss" methods. We need to define clearly what sort of maturity we want to see in the children, and then work out how to lead them there.[48]

Lorna feels that the equipping is best run by the parents, rather than the church. The equipping gives the parents a set of guidelines to help the children in their path toward maturity. Lorna knows, however, that many parents feel inadequate in taking their children through the equipping and that the church plays an important role in both equipping the parents and those children from non-Christian homes.

For those children without Christian parents, Jenkins recommends that a sponsor is chosen who functions as a spiritual parent to guide the child through the equipping. Here are the basic stages:

Stage One of the Equipping Track

- Step 1. Decision time. During this step, the parents or sponsor guides the child to receive Jesus. The books *Now I Follow Jesus* and *Treasure Hunt* are used.
- Step 2. Discovering the child's spiritual experience. The parents or sponsor finds out how much the child knows about the Christian life. This stage includes discovering problems and bondages in the child's life.

- Step 3. Basic discipling. The child understands the implications of following Jesus. The parents or sponsor guide the child to become a disciple of Jesus by using the book *Now I Follow Jesus*.
- Step 4. Daily time with God. The child learns how to know God through reading the Bible and other spiritual disciplines. The book *Living Life Upside Down* is used.

Stage Two of the Equipping Track

- Step 1. Cell group participation. The child joins a cell group and begins to understand the importance of cell participation.
- Step 2. Christian family values. Both parents and children are taught how to have family devotions together.
- Step 3. Understanding and sharing the Lord's supper. Children are taught to take the Lord's supper with their parents in the cell group.
- Step 4. Evangelism. The book *Breaking the Barrier* helps children to share their faith and to guide them in leading a person to know Jesus Christ as Lord and Savior.

Stage Three of the Equipping Track

Usually a child is in the upper elementary years when starting this phase, although there are no hard and fast rules. These courses are offered by the staff in the church.

- Step 1. Spiritual formation. This course covers key Christian truths on a more in-depth level. Baptism follows the course after completing the book, *Spiritual Formation*. The children discuss topics such as:

-What is salvation?
-Can we know we are saved?
-What is baptism?

-What does it mean to live in the Holy Spirit?
-Identity in Christ
-Stewardship
-Worship
-FCBC's style of church and its vision

Before the course is finished, the child is asked to write out his or her testimony. The cell group must recommend the child for baptism.

- Step 2. Sermon notes. Older children keep a notebook to record sermon notes. The kids share with the other children at the cell group what they have written down about the sermon. When the child has taken sermon notes for eight sermons, he or she has completed this step.

- Step 3. Spiritual warfare. Children are taught about the realities of spiritual attack. The book *Victory in Jesus* is used. Topics include:

-The nature of the battle
-Spiritual realm
-The armor of God
-Dealing with temptation
-Spiritual gifts
-Ministering in the power of the Holy Spirit
-Strategic prayer warfare

The children attend this class at the recommendation of the cell group.

- Step 4. Bible overview. Many children know a lot of Bible stories, but they don't know how the Bible comes together.

In this course they are taught more systematically about the Bible.

Lorna Jenkins writes, "The vision of our children's ministry is to produce children who attain full Christian maturity according to their age. Our goal is that they should be worship leaders, prayer warriors, evangelists, sponsors, team leaders, and ministry helpers. The equipping track is our means of achieving this goal."[49] Later reflecting on her years at FCBC, Lorna writes,

> Looking back I can see the startling results in the lives of the children, who were mature Christians for their age and were practicing the Christian life and ministry by the time they were early teens. I have been back to Singapore two years ago and found many of those kids now grown up and taking leadership in the life of the church. They were "golden children."[50]

THE VINE CHURCH'S EQUIPPING

The Vine Church has a constant need to prepare new leaders as they now have some 10,000 children's cell groups and many of the new groups will be led by those who are now children. Along with developing the children in cell and celebration, the Vine also equips the children through their step-by-step discipleship equipping.

First, they ask the children to go to a three-day Encounter retreat. The children at the Vine start going to the Encounter when they are seven years old. These Encounters start on Friday and finish on Sunday afternoon. They take place every weekend in the mother church. Many are transformed, receive prophetic words, and even speak in tongues. After the Encounter, the children continue to receive discipleship through the weekly cell and celebration.

When the child is twelve, he or she can be baptized in water and continue taking the normal equipping course, which is called the Winner's Path:

1. Encounter retreat
2. Living Water course
3. Baptism
4. Consolidation course
5. Spiritual maturity course
6. Leaders training course

The Vine Church doesn't rush baptism. They want to make sure the child is ready. They realize that some parents wrongfully rush their children into baptism on the erroneous assumption that the children might otherwise be eternally lost. The Vine believes, however, that baptism should only be for those who can understand the commitment that is involved. Those in the equipping finish the process when they are teenagers, and are then ready to lead a cell group when they turn sixteen years old.

KEY PRINCIPLES WHEN EQUIPPING CHILDREN

Discipleship equipping for children varies from church to church, depending on doctrine, denomination, and values. Equipping also varies with regard to methodology (e.g., variety of Encounter retreats, one-on-one, classroom instruction, and so forth). Yet there are important principles that should be kept in mind when ministering to children.

STORYTELLING

Ministry to children needs to be based squarely on God's Word with the goal of transformation, rather than simply information. But how is that best done? How can we make the Bible relevant to children?

Storytelling is one of the best ways to teach children, and there are a lot of stories in the Bible. In fact, God loves stories. Christian educators, Choun and Lawson note,

> In doing the work of the church, Christians today usually preach sermons and provide answers. Jesus, on the other hand, told stories and asked questions. To his listeners, the setting and situations he described were familiar. His probing questions led listeners to think about each lesson's application to their own lives.[51]

Like Jesus, children love to hear and tell stories. I remember how my own children would love to hear my mother weave a story together that would have my kids enthralled. They just listened and marveled at how their grandmother could tell a story about them but with other names and characters and always bring it back to a moral principle. When they became older, such stories didn't hold the same magic, but when they were younger, they couldn't get enough stories from their grandmother.

C. S. Lewis had such a significant impact on children because he realized that children love to explore the make-believe world, and Lewis excelled at crafting creative stories that won over their imagination and kept them coming back for more. Ivy Beckwith writes,

I don't know for sure why God gave us all these stories, but I suspect it has something to do with the way we human beings are created. God knew there was something in the human spirit that could relate to, inhabit, and be transformed by stories, even stories conceived thousands of years before in dramatically different cultures from those of the hearers. And I think God gave us stories because God wants us to know God's essence and to fall in love with God. I don't know about you, but it is far easier for me to fall in love with a character in a story than with an exhortation or list of theological propositions about that character. I think God wanted to capture our imaginations, and the way to capture most people's imaginations is through a good story.[52]

I found myself weeping recently as I read the story of Joseph in Genesis when he revealed himself to his brothers. I felt so deeply when Jacob, the father with his own troubled life, embraced Joseph after thinking he was dead for so many years. Stories have a powerful way of gripping us deeply and revealing important lessons that mere propositional truth rarely penetrates.

Once the teacher tells a story based on Scripture, it's also important to lead the children to make a simple conclusion about what they have learned. They need to reflect on the story, hear what they received from the story, and then determine how it applies to their lives. God is working in the lives of children to help them to process God's truth in their lives. We need to allow them to process those thoughts and apply God's Word to their lives right now.

It's important that the listeners are comfortable and can clearly see the person telling the story. Younger listeners tend to creep up on the teacher during the story. An intimacy will be established between teller and listener by eye contact and interaction. To preserve this, keep the group small and keep smaller listeners up front.[53]

Storytelling is not just about stories from the Bible, but it also refers to personal testimony. We need to freely share what God has done in our own lives, and this speaks deeply to children as well. Beckwith says, "We need to allow space for children to explore the story in ways that are meaningful to them."[54] Some of my fondest memories were having personal devotions with my kids. I loved that time so much because I was able to share my "story" and then to make sure each of them had time to talk about what they learned from Scripture and what they needed prayer for.

ACTION

Children unravel a lot of who they are through spontaneous play. We might view them as whittling away their time with idle play, but those spontaneous role playing times are critical in their learning about life and applying knowledge they receive from others. Evelyn M. R. Johnson and Bobbie Bower write,

> A great privilege of childhood is spontaneous play. It is a powerful vehicle to help children understand their world. It helps children reduce stress, sort out life's relationships, and practice emerging skills and abilities. Adults often see play as opportunities to escape the responsibilities and reality of life. For children, play is their life. The power to play, without guilt, is the one part of childhood that adults often regret losing.[55]

Children constantly acquire new experiences and find satisfaction and meaning in play, games, sports, performance, laughter, the senses, the imagination, personal growth, and learning. Play is also the way children process their inner fears and conflicts, including that innate fear of the power of adults.

They cannot work out their fears intellectually but often do so through play. Verbal processing doesn't work for children as it does for adults. Their verbal expression is not yet deep enough or extensive enough to handle the job. They don't have a broad range of knowledge and observation upon which to draw. So they dramatize their conflicts, then bring them under control—enact them and then vanquish them. Play is hard work.[56] David Cohen and Stephen A. MacKeith write,

> Children spend a great deal of their time playing. Some, but not all, play involves imaginative acts. Pretend play in which children act out a variety of often swiftly changing roles is the most obvious form of creative play.[57]

Often their play seems disorganized, but to them it's perfectly natural. Childhood is unique in that there is much more new information generated from experience than there is old information that has been acquired from experience. Assimilation and accommodation are much more complex processes during childhood than during adulthood.[58] Children generate this new information as they play with their friends. It's a fascinating time of adventure and exploration of new territory. Wes Haystead writes, "The most effective way for a child to learn is through firsthand experiences."[59]

Life explodes around a child, and they experience every minute of it. In comparison, adults are boring. Notice this dialogue about doing "nothing" from the perspective of a child:

> We went home and when somebody said, "Where were you?" we said, "out," and when somebody said, "What

were you doing until this hour of the night?" we said, as always, "Nothing."

But about this doing nothing: we swung on swings. We went for walks. We lay on our backs in backyards and chewed grass . . .

We watched things: we watched people build houses, we watched men fix cars, we watched each other patch bicycle tires with rubber bands . . .

We sat in boxes; we sat under porches; we sat on roofs; we sat on limbs of trees.

We stood on boards over excavations; we stood on tops of piles of leaves; we stood under rain dripping from the eaves; we stood up to our ears in snow.

We looked at things like knives and jimmies and pig nuts and grasshoppers and clouds and dogs and people.

We skipped and hopped and jumped. Not going anywhere—just skipping and hopping and jumping and galloping.

We sang and whistled and hummed and screamed. We did a lot of nothing.[60]

What we think is a lot of "nothing" in the life of a child is really a world exploding with excitement and adventure. Children can make castles in the sand and adventure in an asphalt playground. They love to dance, talk, eat, and laugh. What adults might think of as "nothing" can be a dream world for children.

Knowing this will help leaders remember that children delight in experiencing Christ's teaching through play-acting. As much as possible, help them to interact with the teaching through role playing.

I remember when my children were young, they could dramatize anything, and they loved to perform in front of others. I was amazed at their creativity and role playing ability. They didn't understand details about detective work, but they were ready to become Sherlock Holmes through role playing. Yet as I reflect back on many of those occasions, I now realize that they were learning valuable lessons and solidifying knowledge. They never would have been able to do this by taking notes in a classroom or reflecting on what they learned in a group. Diana Shmukler writes,

> Not only do children need time and opportunity, but they also need wealth of content for their fantasy play. As such, a second requirement is the availability of a variety of materials in the form of stories told, books and playthings which increase the likelihood that the material presented to the child will be sufficiently interesting and novel to engage and hold their interest and attention with pleasure. Children also need an environment that is not too structured or well-ordered so they can develop great flexibility in using the material at hand.[61]

We need to feed their dreams and encourage their play. After teaching a Bible story, it's a good idea to allow the children to act it out. Giving them this opportunity will help them achieve a balance between inner and outer experience and provide an important sense of self-esteem. As Diana Shmukler notes,

By its very nature, play demands that children use their potential to combine experiences into organized, yet flexible schemes. It is thus a powerful adjunct to early educational preventive and therapeutic procedures and, as such, should be central in any preschool activity.[62]

Wise teachers explain the Bible stories but then allow the children to internalize the message through play acting. And this can take place in cell, celebration, as well as discipleship equipping.

SPIRITUALITY

Some act as if spirituality is reserved only for adults. But what about children? Are they spiritual as well? Actually, spirituality comes quite naturally for children, whereas adults often struggle more in the area of spirituality. Child researcher, Rebecca Nye, believes that children have an advantage when it comes to spirituality because they have a more holistic way of seeing things; they don't analyze as much, so their perception has a more mystical quality.[63]

George Müller, the builder of the famous Christian orphan houses of Bristol, England, in the nineteenth century, is an example of a person who took seriously the spirituality of children. Muller engaged in prayer for revival among the children. In January and February, 1860, a mighty wave of the Holy Spirit's power swept over the institution. It began among the little girls, from six to nine years old, then extended to the older girls, and then to the boys, until, more than two hundred were seeking after God and finding peace with him.

The young converts at once asked to hold prayer meetings among themselves, and many began to pray for others. Out of the 700 orphans, some 260 were converted or in a "hopeful state." The record indicates that these kids did not merely confess "I want to be baptized," but they had a faith that was based on a genuine experience with the Spirit of God. They quickly put that faith into action on behalf of other children. Sadly, some adults might minimize a child's tears of repentance, thinking the child doesn't have much to repent from.

Ralph Neighbour remembers a story from the 1990s when Lorna Jenkins directed the children's cells at FCBC. A man came in a wheel chair, asking for prayer. The adults prayed fervently for him, without any observable healing. The adults drifted into the kitchen for refreshments, leaving the man and an 8-year-old girl behind. The child stared at the man and finally said, "Well, why don't you get up and walk?" The Spirit of God fell on him at that moment and he rose up and walked into the kitchen. Astonished, the adults asked, "What happened?" "It was the little girl! She told me to walk." When the adults queried the girl, she simply said, "Well, you all prayed for him. So I just told him to walk because he was healed."[64]

However we choose to define spirituality, we know that children have a lot of it. They are very blessed with the capacity to be sensitive to God. They are open to what God would say to them, and they are willing to listen and obey.[65] Those leading children in cell ministry or teaching them in the discipleship equipping should get the children involved in praying for one another, listening to the voice of God, speaking out what they hear, and evangelizing those who don't know Jesus.

GET R.E.A.L.

Children say what they feel and act out what they say. They exemplify authenticity and genuine transparency. This is how God made them. When teaching children, the acronym REAL goes a long way in learning what works with children:

Relational: Children can be friends with anyone. This is their nature. Most adults observing children interacting with their close friends can easily see these special bonds in action. The best teachers enjoy the relational interaction with children and transmit this loving vitality in their teaching.

Experiential: Children love hands-on learning. They love to be involved in their learning. I remember doing finger painting in Mrs. Westcott's class in kindergarten. It involved all of me, and I relished the experience. I felt the same exhilaration working with the building blocks or playing on the playground. The best teachers, in fact, stimulate the children to experience the teaching through role playing, coloring, creating their own stories, worship, prayer, and so forth. Experiences stir the creative energy in children as well as solidifying the biblical teaching.

Applicable: Apply the lesson to the child's real world. Long, boring "exegetical" teaching just doesn't work with kids. They need to see what you're doing. Become an actor. Live your teaching message. I remember in Bible school we had an instructor named Alban Douglas. He was the favorite teacher in the school because he acted out his lessons. He would dramatize Old Testament stories to make sure we felt and could imagine what actually happened back then. The goal was always application. Of course, we were adult Bible students.

How much more important for children to see, experience, and apply biblical truth.

Learner based: Base your teaching around the learners, not the teachers. Think about their interests, their learning styles, and their attention spans. Children are remarkably sensitive to the expressions of the human voice. By the time they reach school age, most children can imitate the melody of anger, of fear, of delight, and of many other emotions.[66]

Working with children is a wonderful experience because they live in God's realm—the realm of joy and creativity. Make sure that the teaching in the cell, equipping, and celebration is full of life, interaction, and hands-on learning.

Chapter 8
EQUIPPING THE PARENTS

At MCM in Barquisimeto, Venezuela, many of the cell groups are led by adolescents, who regularly have their devotional time, visit members of their cell, prepare the lesson, pray for the sick, and experience God's miracles in the group. Jose, an adolescent leader said, "God is doing great things in my cell group. My friends are coming to Jesus and lives are being changed." Patricia, an adolescent leader sitting next to José, agreed. "I pray and God guides me." Patricia said.

Yet, as I talked to the staff who were also present in that meeting, they told me about the difficulties that confronted them. "Our church has made incredible strides, but we need the parents' support, and many are still resistant. The main hindrance is getting the parents to open their homes, take their children to the cells, and allow us to prepare the adolescents as well as the children to do the work of the ministry."

After talking with these leaders at MCM, I realized afresh that children's cell ministry depends on parents who are committed and ready to get involved. Children don't have cars. They don't have finances. They can't open their own homes. Ministry to children, in other words, is largely dependent on adults.

Parents are vital in the cell system but more importantly in their own homes—in the inner cell. So parents need to be taught how to develop their own children through exemplifying Christ-like behavior, leading their children in family devotions, and spending sufficient time with their kids, showing them their true priorities.

The reality, however, is that many children do not have Christian parents, so the church fulfills the role of spiritual parent. Anna Mow writes, "The church also has its unique responsibility to the children. The church must finish what the family cannot do, and it must compensate for wherever the family fails the children."[67]

I am coaching one church planter who told me about neighborhood children coming to his house each week. "One girl has been transformed through our house church," the pastor told me. "She is talking to her non-Christian parents about Jesus," he said. In the absence of godly parents, the Bend Community Church is discipling her, preparing her for the future, and in the process reaching her non-Christian parents.

WE'VE NEVER DONE IT THIS WAY BEFORE

When introducing a new idea, there is always a push back. The fallback mode is the way it was done in the past. Of course, there will always be early adapters and those who love change, but it seems that most people like it the way it has always been—the good old days. Pastors and leaders need to be ready to face common areas of resistance, like the ones mentioned below.

THE FORGETTING THE FUTURE BARRIER

It's easy to forget that children will soon be youth, young adults, and adults. If the children are involved now in cell ministry, there is a much better chance they will continue the process when they get older. Without those early seeds of vibrant ministry, it's much harder for them to simply jump in later on.

In a blink of an eye, dependent children are responsible adults. To prepare children in the process of maturing, parents need to look beyond their children as babies and small children to the time when those same children play an important role in the church as leaders, pastors, and missionaries. If the children are not involved right now in the local church, why will they suddenly get involved in the future?

Since house to house ministry is the New Testament norm for making disciples who make disciples, shouldn't parents want to make sure their children are also involved in that environment now? By allowing the children to be involved now in cell ministry, there's a far greater likelihood that they will be involved later, as they go from the children's cells to youth cells, and on to adult cell ministry.

THE FAITH BARRIER

One barrier to break in the minds of parents is the faith roadblock. I'm referring to the fact that many parents don't believe that their children have the ability to lead others to Jesus, make disciples, and change the world in the process. They view their children as listeners but not potential ministers. Some parents want to wait until their children are old enough to be involved in church ministry. But by that time it's too late. One of the reasons that youth are leaving the church in droves is because they were only viewed as passive listeners when they were children, rather than active participants.

Some parents doubt that children can participate in a cell group. They are afraid that the children cannot form genuine and confidential relationships with adults in an IG setting. Even though this is not true, it's part of the barrier that needs to be removed for adults to wholeheartedly get involved in children's ministry.

THE INVOLVEMENT BARRIER

Sometimes parents lack a clear understanding of their role in developing children. Perhaps they think the schools or churches will do the job for them. They think that their role only involves providing for their children's physical needs. Someone else is supposed to supply the children's spiritual and educational needs. The reality is that parents have the first and foremost role in equipping their children spiritually. They are also responsible to make sure their children receive additional help in the church.

Serving children requires voluntary sacrifice and service because they can't give back anything financially right now. But children will give back in the future. Parents need to be reminded that they will receive their payment in other ways very soon. Children give back by their love, their simplicity, and their honesty. The motivation to serve them now is God's honor and reward. The payback will be their transformed character and spiritual lives. It's also true that children's cell groups are time consuming and labor intensive. Parents must be willing to find the time to participate and minister.

BUSYNESS BARRIER

Often parents are so busy that they neglect the development of their children. Beckwith writes,

> Today's families struggle with the irregular and erratic schedules of various family members. Dad and/or Mom may be gone a significant part of the day, working to keep food on the table. The evening meal is fast food in the car as families run to a variety of afternoon and early evening commitments. These activities, which are probably good in themselves, can pull families apart rather than fuel closer relationships.[68]

Parents need to provide for their children and working hard to pay the bills is the right thing to do. But many parents work the extra hours to possess more gadgets and things—the luxuries of this world—rather than to provide for the basic needs of their family. Little time is left over for their spiritual training.

It's always encouraging when parents stop and reexamine their priorities. I talked with one missionary who told me that his dad, an international minister, stopped his ministry for one year to spend time with him during his troubled years. His dad had become too busy with Christian work while his son slipped away from the Lord. The dad was willing, however, to admit his error and change. I admire this father's commitment to place the well-being of his child above his own ministerial success. Sadly, many do not. Rather, they place their own success in life over their relationship with their children.

Wise pastors and leaders understand the need to prepare the ground through biblical teaching to prepare the parents to participate in children's cell ministry. And yes, there will be some initial resistance.

CHANGING THE ATTITUDES

So how can these attitudes change? What can the church do to turn parents into frontline workers and helpers in cell church ministry?

PRAYING

Only God can change attitudes and grant long-term success. Unseen values run deep in the leaders and gatekeepers. People might agree to develop the children, but deep down, they know that new commitments—whatever they are—might take away time and energy from their own ministries and programs. Satan is quick to stir up strife through backbiting and internal resistance, and often the leaders won't even know where it's coming from.

Fervent prayer, therefore, is needed to counteract the fiery darts of the devil, since Satan is 100% opposed to discipling the next generation. Pastors and leaders must remember Paul's exhortation in Ephesians 6:12, "For our struggle is not against flesh and blood, but against the rulers, against the authorities, against the powers of this dark world and against the spiritual forces of evil in the heavenly realms."

Recently in my own local church, we went through a very tough period in which a couple became divisive through subtle backbiting. We tried to resolve the situation through the biblical mandate of Matthew 18, talking directly to the person, then two or three, then the church. But the couple finally left and caused turmoil in the church. What did the leadership learn? We learned the need to redouble our prayer effort. We had let down the guard. We needed to pray more.

When changing attitudes among parents to prioritize children, prayer needs to be the first weapon, the first place to start. God loves children, so he is on their side. He desires that the church prioritize the discipleship of children through cell and celebration. For this reason, the church can pray with confidence, boldly approaching the throne of grace and believing that God will help the parents to get involved in this new focus (1 John 5:14-15).

LEADING THE CHARGE

Leadership is critical. Aluizio and Marcia Silva at the Vine Church have consistently promoted the development of children for the last fifteen years. Today, they have a vibrant children's ministry that is influencing the world. But it didn't happen overnight. They had to preach about the biblical foundation for children and faithfully guide the process. Change didn't come quickly or easily. They constantly had to remind the church of the biblical reasons for children's ministry and the heavenly rewards for serving Jesus. Fast forward fifteen years, and many of those children are now leaders in the church. Making disciples of children is now a way of life at the Vine, but it wasn't always that way. And it still takes work to quell doubt and maintain the vision.

Mario Vega regularly teaches about the priority of children and the need to prepare them now. One of his seminar topics is children in cell ministry. He has invested a lot of time into developing the discipleship equipping for children's cell leaders. Those in the church quickly grasp that Mario is passionate about developing children and committed to prioritizing them in both cell and celebration. Elim members know that preparing to lead a children's cell is important to God, the lead pastor, and the church's long-term vision.

Pastor Keison at MCM in Venezuela breathes the children's vision. From the moment I entered the church, I knew their priority—to prepare for the future by discipling the children. I heard the story of his trip to Wales on various occasions—and not just from pastor Keison but from his leadership team. The leadership encouraged me to see videos of children's ministry in action, talk to adolescents leading cell groups, and take home their literature. My purpose for being in the church was to teach the adults about cell ministry, but I left with a clarity and excitement about prioritizing the children.

SPEAKING THE VISION

Vision casting plays an important part in prioritizing children's ministry. In the beginning of this book, I laid out the biblical basis for placing a priority on discipling children, both in the home as well as in the cell-based church. As the pastor highlights the biblical basis for making disciples of children, the congregation will understand the divine motivation for children's ministry. The pastor will need to cast the vision to the leadership team, to cell members during special gatherings, and to those gathered on Sunday morning. The goal is that parents will slowly begin to prioritize their own involvement in opening their homes, ensuring their children are going through the equipping, taking their children with them to the cell groups, and driving their children to cell groups when they themselves are not involved

Along with preaching God's Word is the need to recognize those who are ministering to children in both the cell and celebration. Paul says in 1 Thessalonians 5:12, ". . . appreciate those who diligently labor among you . . ." (New American Standard Version). The Greek word literally means to perceive or to know those who labor. Recognition means acknowledging the diligent labors of children's leaders, those ministering in the Kids' Slot, or teaching the children in the equipping or larger celebration gathering. The purpose of recognition is to honor and affirm the hard work and labor of those ministering to children.

EXEMPLIFYING

The old saying is true, "put your money where your mouth is." If children are a priority, the church needs to budget money for ministry to children. I'm referring to budgeting money for materials, staff, and equipping. Robert Lay's ministry, for example, has developed an excellent set of materials for churches wanting to connect cell, celebration, and the home. Yet, those materials cost money and churches need to be willing to set aside monies in the budget to buy those materials each year.

Paul said, "Follow my example, as I follow the example of Christ" (1 Cor. 11:1). Brian Kannel, lead pastor of YAC, personally leads an IG group. His own example speaks volumes to those in the church. He is able to connect sermon illustrations with his own cell, which helps stir others to get involved. The power of example is a strong stimulus to stir parents to follow his lead.

Pastor Keison and Belkys at MCM have not only built their church around children but their family also prioritizes children, having adopted eight orphans. They are living the life they want others to follow.

EQUIPPING THE FAMILY CIRCLE

While it's important to help parents to get involved in children's ministry in the local church, it's even more important that parents care for their children at home. I call this the inner cell, the family cell. This small, inside group should get the highest priority. Scripture is clear, "Train a child in the way he should go, and when he is old he will not turn from it" (Prov. 22:6). The writer of Proverbs is talking directly to the parents in this verse. Paul also places the responsibility on parents when he says, "Fathers, do not exasperate your children; instead, bring them up in the training and instruction of the Lord" (Eph. 5:4).

I disagree with those who teach that the church is more responsible than parents to disciple the children. I believe the order is clear: God first, spouse second, and family third. Church ministry comes later. And one of the critical roles of the church is to equip the parents to develop their own children. Mike Sciarra writes,

> We need to re-educate parents about their roles as their children's primary faith-shapers. Many parents lack the confidence and skills to comfortably take a leadership role. You'll know if it's working if your stress level decreases,

your joy in ministry increases, and you have people on your team who are excited about the same things you are![69]

The church's equipping should be directed toward helping the parents live the gospel in front of their children. Granted, not all children come from Christian homes and sometimes the church must assume the role of a parent in developing children's spiritual lives. Yet, an essential role of the church is to teach the parents about how to model the Christian faith at home.

Parents are on the front lines in modeling Christianity to their children and letting them see up-close that Jesus is alive through their lifestyles. Christian education expert, Lawrence O. Richards, writes,

> Those children who believed that God was real to their parents had a sense of personal relationship with Him. Those children who sensed that God was not real to their parents saw Him as a person who was "a tradition," who "is hardly ever talked about," and who just "doesn't matter."[70]

As Richards researched children from Christian homes who continued to follow Jesus, he noted, "Somehow the parents' faith was caught, and even those who had all the right information about God and could score perfect papers on a test about what He is like did not feel they knew Him unless they sensed that somehow God was real to mom and dad."[71] This idea of being "real to mom and dad" is the frontline witness to children and what will have a far greater impact than all the preaching and teaching combined.

UNPLANNED MODELING SHAPED THE CHILDREN

Throughout the Old Testament and in Deuteronomy more specifically, we see that parents were to mold and shape their children through the unplanned and natural situations of life (Deut. 6:1, 2, 3, 17, 18). The parents were specifically reminded that religious education was a day-by-day thing which happened at any time, in any place, even during those moments they were unaware of their influence. The church needs to constantly remind parents that the most effective teaching is lifestyle.

Attending church on Sunday and cell group during the week will help adults grow in the Lord, but it's their daily lives lived out before their children that will make the difference. Vernon Anderson writes:

> Christian education cannot be very effective without the co-operation of the home. Values rub off on children. The unspoken word, the casual remark, and the behavior of parents make deep impressions upon children . . . The home—the center of the child's world—exists in a community.[72]

It's best for children to see their parents' own joy at worshipping and obeying the Lord of creation. As children see their parents spending time with God, they will also respond to the Savior. Once children have this kind of understanding of God, they will be prepared to endure the seductive tensions of the world.

The opposite is also true. I know two boys who were brought up in a "Christian home." These two boys were often in my home, played with my own children, and we had many conversations about God and life in general. Yet as the years passed, these two boys became atheists. The primary reason was because of a dad who failed to live his faith. This father knew Jesus, understood the Word, but wasn't transformed by the gospel. He was a bad example in the home, disrespected his wife, and could not control his cursing and judgmental spirit. He was quick to label and judge. His oppressive example soured his children to the Christian faith. These two boys made a choice to become atheists and will be held accountable to God for their actions. Yet, what they saw—or didn't see in their dad's lifestyle—fueled their unbelief.

Parents must realize that their primary role is to prepare their children now, while they are teachable, available, and moldable. Soon they will be on their own in a world that is often hostile to the gospel. The apostle John says, "We know that we are children of God, and that the whole world is under the control of the evil one" (1 John 5:20). Parents need to view those early years as a time of preparing children for the unbelieving world full of ungodly thinking. One of the church's primary roles, therefore, is to prepare parents to disciple their own children and prepare them to love and serve Jesus.

What children see in those early years is more important than what they hear. They learn more from what adults do than from what adults say; they are sensitive to the hidden curriculum. Educators call this "informal education. In the early years, informal education primarily takes place in the home and has more of a direct impact than the formal teaching offered in church or schools. Informal education is the lifelong process in which attitudes, values, skills, and knowledge are acquired from daily experience and educational resources in the child's environment. The common phrase "values are more caught than taught" is a reference to the informal education children experience in families and other social networks and are absorbed into their behaviors and foundational attitudes.[73]

The church's role is to prepare the parents to live the Christian lives in front of their children, rather than expecting the church to do it for them. Mike Sciarra writes,

> Parents are an afterthought to many children's pastors. Yes, we sincerely want to make a difference in the lives of our children's families—to help parents become more intentional about teaching their children, for instance. But our response to that desire is to tack on one more program that doesn't include both parents and children.[74]

Rather than an afterthought, the equipping of parents needs to be a priority. Not only should parents hear this from the pulpit, but cell groups need to be encouraged to talk about successes and failures of parenting. Cell groups are intimate environments where transparency should be prioritized. During the cell lesson or prayer time afterwards, parents need to be able to say, "Pray for me, I need to control my anger. I know this is negatively affecting my marriage, but it's also sending the wrong signals to my children."

RECIPROCAL MINISTRY

Although parents have a primary role in shaping their children, the process of discipleship is mutual. Children are often God's instruments to shape and "disciple" the parents. Michael Ferris, an educator and author who successfully raised three daughters, wrote a book called *What a Daughter Needs from Her Dad*. He says:

> From a very early age your daughter will know when you have made the wrong decision, snapped to an inappropriate judgment. . . A father who refuses to admit a mistake or

to work at changing poor, immature behavior reaps a daughter who refuses to trust him. . . Your reliability is actually enhanced when you are willing to admit to the evident fact that you have made a mistake.[75]

The church needs to encourage parents to admit their mistakes when children point them out. It's a far better choice and builds respect. Johnson and Bower write,

> Children bring out the best and worst in adults. Their situations can produce intense frustration or delight; profound sorrow or joy. With children in their midst, adults find fresh meaning in the phrase "child of God" and in what it means to live out that loving, tender relationship.[76]

When parents speak respectfully to each other, children grow up with that same respect in their conversations. Those who watch mommy and daddy enjoying books often develop a love for reading. They internalize values as they see and live them. Children notice, in detail, what adults do. Early on they become aware of any difference between what parents teach them and how parents act.

On her way to a church event, a pastor's wife needed to pick something up at a downtown office. "Pray that we'll find a parking place right in front of the office, honey," she said to her daughter. When they arrived, there was one parking space in front of the office—but another car had begun turning in to it. Undaunted, the pastor's wife nosed into the space and cheerfully turned off the car. "But Mommy," her daughter exclaimed in disbelief, "he was turning in here." "We prayed for a place, didn't we? It's ours," her mother responded. More than fifty years later, that daughter remembers her disappointment over her mother's lack of integrity.

Children are troubled by double standards and lose respect for parents who continue to demand of them what they are unwilling to do themselves. Those parents who listen to their children and take a look at themselves through the eyes of their children, will grow in humility, dependence on God, and maturity in the Christian walk. In some cases, parents need to relax the standards set for their children, knowing that they themselves are not living the life they expect of them.

Those times that children wake up and see their mom or dad reading God's Word, interceding for a lost world, or listening to worship music will make a lasting impression on the child. The opposite is also true. If they rarely see their parents spending time with God, they will not be encouraged to do it themselves. Or at least they won't consider the quiet time as being a priority. Worse yet, if they hear their parents teaching others about the priority of the quiet time but then see a double standard at home, they will be turned off to the gospel.

Children need to discover through observation that Christianity is not primarily practiced on Sunday in a church building: God is important to the adults they love all week long at home and at work. Children are blessed when families enjoy God together. Music that celebrates God's goodness may draw the family into God's presence as it provides a backdrop for life or screens out distracting noises so that a little one can fall asleep. And in regular or special times of prayer, families can invite and enjoy God's presence. Children are also deeply influenced by how the significant adults in their lives respond to unexpected events.

A lot of those significant teaching moments come because of trials. In times of stress and grief, do children see the parents turning to God and God's people for strength and guidance? Are the parents willing to process with the children the hard questions about God and pain? In war and tragedy, do they hear the parents praying for all those who suffer, including enemies? In other words, it's critical that children see a real faith being refined in the crucible of life. One single mother said, "All my kids have a real understanding of God because we're a family that lives by faith. There have been times when we've just been hanging on by our teeth and I've said, 'OK, God, there's nothing I can do,' and God always comes through. The kids know that."[77]

EQUIPPING IN THE SPIRITUAL DISCIPLINES

The church needs to equip parents in the area of prayer. Parents need to be reminded that they are in a spiritual battle (Eph. 6:12). Satan would love to sidetrack the children to follow the ways of the world and parents are the primary prayer warriors to stand in the gap for them.

To help ensure this happens, it's essential that the church equip parents on how to spiritually wrestle for their children through prayer on a personal basis, but also how to have a daily quiet time.

The family quiet time is the best time for parents to nurture children in the ways of God and really prepare them for life with Christ. The church should encourage the parents to have devotions with their children every day. Parents can play a life-changing role in discipling their children through a daily quiet time. It's like having a cell group with children each day, in which parent(s) and children can worship, talk about personal struggles, meditate on God's Word, and even ask their children to hear and respond to God's voice. Some parents prefer to follow a devotional guide while other parents will create their own. The main focus is to help children develop their own sensitivity to God and hear the voice of Jesus for themselves.

The church needs to also equip parents to take a day off each week. Many churches avoid this topic, perhaps because their emphasis is on tasks and busy ministry work. Yet a God-honoring church prioritizes equipping the parents to minister to their own families first and only secondarily to serving in the church. Taking a day off is essential—both for parents and family members. It gives the family a chance to have fun, gather strength, and face the day with new vigor. It helps the family build and maintain strong relationships. Plato once wrote, "You can learn more about a man in an hour of play than in a year of conversation."[78]

STARTING WITH THE MARRIAGE

One of the most important things the church can do is equip the parents to have healthy marriages. Healthy children, healthy cells, and healthy churches all share a common foundation—strong marriages. Children feel cared for and loved when the husband and wife live in harmony. The husband and wife relationship is the glue that makes the other relationships work. The greatest thing a father can do for his children is to love his wife.

My wife Celyce and I know through experience that when we are doing well, our children feel secure. When I make my wife feel special, my kids honor me in a special way. Developing an intimate relationship with Celyce is one of the greatest gifts I can give to my children.

One Christian friend who suffered a divorce recalled his son asking during the divorce proceedings, "Where is God in all this, Dad?" The son still hasn't recovered. The glue of marriage, which was supposed to help this boy grow in his relationship with God, unraveled. One reason why God hates divorce is because the children suffer in the process. Malachi says,

> Has not the LORD made them one? In flesh and spirit they are his. And why one? Because he was seeking godly offspring. So guard yourself in your spirit, and do not break faith with the wife of your youth. "I hate divorce," says the LORD God of Israel, "and I hate a man's covering himself with violence as well as with his garment," says the LORD Almighty. So guard yourself in your spirit, and do not break faith (Mal. 2:15-16).

God desires for kids to see community lived out between father and mother. When this is not the case, insecurity develops. Often bitterness surfaces toward the parent because of the vague hopelessness the child feels about his or her own prospects in developing close relationships with friends and a future spouse. Inconsistent parents produce insecure children. God is looking for godly offspring as parents prioritize a loving relationship with each other and their children.[79]

The church is called to equip husbands and wives through biblical teaching, discipleship equipping, and even focusing on marriage in the cell group. A church, for example, might teach for seven weeks on marriage and then apply those messages in the cell group, where the people can respond about their own marriages. Another church did a five-week series on marriage connected with a famous video series on that topic. The cell groups watched the 30-minute video each week and answered questions. After the five-week series concluded, the groups continued with the normal sermon based messages. The church's role, therefore, is to equip parents, whether they are single or married.

Churches should be creative in equipping the parents, asking the Holy Spirit for wisdom to do a better job. Equipping in the cell church extends to the celebration, the cell, the church-wide equipping, and to coaching the leaders on how their marriages are progressing.

TAKE THE NEXT STEP

Pastors and leaders can sometimes feel overwhelmed as they equip parents to prioritize discipling their children. But it's important to remember that the first step doesn't have to be a big one. My advice to pastors and leaders is to start small. I remind them that they don't—and won't—have everything figured out when they start. But it's far more serious to fail to try. The next chapter will articulate a series of steps, with the goal of making the transition to children's cell ministry feasible for pastors and leaders who are contemplating their next move.

_____ Chapter 9 _____
CULTIVATING THE VISION

One pastor wrote me in frustration, "I've tried including the children in our cell ministry for many years and have failed each time. What do I do now?" I shared with him what other churches are doing, some great books on the topic, and general encouragement. Yet, many pastors need more. They would like a step-by-step process for including children in the discipleship process.

Perhaps children in cell ministry is a completely new concept to you. You are not ready to start children's cells because you first need to grasp the vision yourself. But don't stop there.

Make the necessary steps to go from the vision stage to the planning stage to actual implementation.

Wherever you are on the journey, take the step that is most appropriate for you. But do take the necessary step. The famous Chinese maxim holds true: "The journey of a thousand miles begins with a single step." What is the first step you need to take?

STEP 1: ARTICULATE THE VISION

In chapter two, I talked about a new vision for children in cell ministry. Over the last chapters we've seen how others are implementing that strategy. Make sure you start with those values and priorities that will guide your teaching and strategies over the long-haul. Starting children's cell groups just because someone else is doing it won't sustain you when the difficulties come. And they will come. You must have a deep set of convictions and values that you can draw from when problems occur.

I've said over and over and in many different ways that we need to envision children as disciples who can make other disciples, rather than waiting for them to become youth or adults. I've tried to clarify how that cell church ministry is a great way to do this.

You might have a different way of clarifying your vision. The important thing is to take the necessary time to pray and formulate why you want to start prioritizing children. If you're the lead pastor, meet with key team members, whether those team members are cell leaders, elders, or paid staff. Have a retreat. Read Scripture. Determine how you will specifically include children in your overall cell-based vision.

The Vine Church clarifies their vision like this:

1. God is a God of generations. He is concerned that one generation win the next one. We have to pass the baton of faith safely to the next generation, so that our work is not in vain
2. Children are part of the body of Christ. If they are part of the body of Christ, we must not forget them.
3. We must remember that we are raising up a generation of disciples of Christ, and this process starts with the children.

It's wise to clarify your motivation for prioritizing children, just like the Vine Church. As the pastoral team determines the values, these convictions will help the church to know how to invest time, energy, and resources for the children. And then write down the vision. Lorna Jenkins talks about the transition of FCBC to prioritizing children in cell ministry. First there was the need to articulate the vision, but the second step was to write it down to give it more permanency.

STEP 2: PREPARE THE PARENTS AND CHURCH

When FCBC made the transition to IG cells, there was a felt need that the children were not included sufficiently in the life of the church. Some of the reasons were:

- Many families simply handed over their responsibilities to the church.
- The children were still regarded as a separate department in the church.
- The evangelization of children was largely left to the children's leaders.
- Nobody expected very much of the children.

Even though the staff realized there was a need for change, the church leaders had to also convince the parents. Jenkins writes,

> We had to convince the cell groups that it would be good to have the children there. We had to convince parents that their children would not be missing out on their Bible teaching. We had to convince the children that they would not be bored to death. Most of all, we had to convince the children's leaders that the parents could be trusted with the children.[80]

The first step in parental preparation is to go over the biblical truths of children in cell ministry, why it's important, and how children and parents will benefit as a result of this new integration. Parents need to know that children will spend more time with their families in worship and that both parents and children will grow as a result.

Point the parents back to the New Testament house to house ministry, in which the churches were in the home, and children played a vital part. Home cell ministry provides far more opportunity for living out the faith, as children are integrated into the life of the "real" church. They will see their parents actively participating in worship, fellowship, communion, and the Word—not as spectators but as participants.

Some will resist, thinking that the only way to minister to children is by programs and teaching on Sunday. The reality is that cell ministry to children enhances the Sunday teaching by also applying the church's teaching in the weekly cell groups, where the people can ask questions and interact with the teaching.

Secondly, help parents to realize that in a small group, children will experience what it means to be brought up within the context of a family. Faith is caught through quality relationships—not quality programs.

Third, prepare the parents to be hospitable. In practical terms, this means teaching parents about placing people before things, making disciples of children ahead of clean carpets, and viewing the home as a place of ministry rather than a private castle. The reality is that house to house New Testament ministry will require sacrifice. Working with children in homes also requires an ongoing discussion between the parents and church.

Fourth, it's wise to remind parents that children are adaptable and will love the change. The adults are the ones who need to check their view on including children in their church life. Parents should be helping their children make the adjustments, but the whole group must participate in a new, changed attitude toward children. The good news is that the adults will see and hear some wonderful things from the kids.[81]

STEP 3: UNDERSTAND THE PROCESS OF CHANGE

Prioritizing children in cell ministry will take time. Remember the well-worn adage: "Everything takes longer than you expect; even when you expect it to take longer than you expect." In fact, any time something new is introduced into the life of the church, there is the potential for conflict. Introducing IG or CO cells does involve change.

Managing the dynamics of change is one of the most important issues leadership will face in starting or rebuilding the children's ministry. If the changes are handled well, the introduction of IG or CO cells can be a great blessing for the church.

People need time to process ideas. Their heads will nod with enthusiasm when hearing about prioritizing the children in small groups, but often they haven't digested the implications. Remember that different people respond to change at different rates, and that it is not necessarily based on spiritual maturity.

Involving children in cell ministry will take time because people like to maintain the status quo. Once an organization or system gets in motion, it tends to keep going in the same direction. People become comfortable with their traditions and patterns.

Everyone likes something new—for a little while. But when push comes to shove, they'll reach for the old, the established, and the traditional. This is human nature. People might get excited about including children, but when it involves their commitment, like taking children to the cells, it's easy to revert back to old patterns.

I like to use the phrase "programmatic knee jerks" to describe what takes place after the initial change. Suddenly people began to realize that the change will affect them in the practical details of daily living. It might affect the normal children's programming or having to say no to something else in order to find time in the schedule for children. Yes, the system will push back. Expect it.

In the early days of long sea voyages, scurvy (a disease which resulted from a deficiency of vitamin C) killed more sailors than warfare, accidents, and all other causes of death. In 1601, Captain James Lancaster of the British navy conducted an experiment to evaluate the effectiveness of lemon juice in preventing scurvy on four ships. He gave daily portions of lemon juice to the men on one ship while the men aboard the other three ships received nothing. Those on the ship receiving the lemon juice remained healthy while 110 of the 278 men on the other three ships died of scurvy.

The results were so clear that you'd expect the entire British navy to immediately adopt the new cure. Sadly, it wasn't until 1795 (194 years later) that "citrus juice" was adopted as the official cure for scurvy in the British marines. Part of the resistance stemmed from the competing remedies that were offered at the time. Suffice it to say, there were many factors that hindered the full acceptance of the citrus remedy.[82]

Innovation often diffuses slowly. Many factors—often unexplainable—contribute to this resistance. Remember to deal tenderly with those in your church as you present the vision. Give people time to process the new ideas as you carefully explain how the changes will benefit their families. Learning how to manage change dynamics will help you to work through the conflict and establish an effective and long lasting children's ministry in the church.

STEP 4: START WITH A PILOT GROUP

It's a great idea to prototype your first IG or CO group with emotionally healthy adults and children who are more or less stable. Why? Because it's important to start off with a success rather than a failure. The trials will come soon enough, but short term victories will have a positive, lasting psychological effect.

The dictionary defines a prototype as "An original type, form, or instance that serves as a model on which later stages are based or judged." In the early stage of the transition, it is important that other members can see a success and an inspiration for others to follow.

If the church decides to do IG cells, the first one should be led by the person in charge. If the church is just beginning cell ministry, the first IG cell should be led by the lead pastor of the church. If the church already has cell groups but is just starting children's cells, perhaps the wife of the lead pastor will lead it or the person in charge of the children's cell ministry.

Lorna Jenkins explains how FCBC first started their pilot children's group. They practiced a two-part format in which the children were with the adults for the icebreaker and worship. The children then were adjourned to Kids' Slot in another room. They chose to begin the first group in a home where the parents were eager to involve their children. FCBC wanted to make sure that their first pilot group was successful. As they worked out the problems in the first pilot group, multiplied it, and then equipped more leaders, the IG cell vision began to grow and become part of the church's strategy.

Starting a pilot group proclaims that children's cell ministry is better "caught than taught." Rather than starting the transition by "teaching" the people about this new approach, it's best to first allow others to "experience" children's cell ministry. Those initial leaders will then impart to others what they experienced in the initial group. Mistakes made in the prototype stage are more easily corrected before they spread throughout the group system. Key leaders are part of the process from the beginning, making it more likely they will actively support small group ministry. Even Jesus started by forming his own prototype cell. He spent years developing the model. He couldn't afford failure.

After a certain period, the first IG group sends out the original adults with their children to start new IG groups. It's always best to start new groups in at least a team of two. So if there were twelve adults and eight children in the pilot group, perhaps the pilot group could give birth to three or four new IG groups. How long before this happens? I would recommend between six to nine months.

Piloting new groups are important when doing CO groups as well. You will still want to start small, work out the problems, and then develop new groups as the issues are resolved. Perhaps you could start the pilot group at the same time an adult group is taking place, but in another room or area of the house. The initial group should be closely monitored or coached by those in leadership of the children's cell ministry. A team of leaders should lead the initial group with the goal of multiplying new CO groups. The Vine Church started small in the year 2000, made necessary adjustments, and continued to perfect and grow.

Transition is not an easy road, and it's where many churches fail. A vision for children's cell groups requires an entirely different attitude toward children. Not counting the cost and taking the necessary steps to ensure success will result in stagnation and even future resistance.

STEP 5: ADJUST AND PERFECT

You'll never be completely done. You'll simply be in the process of perfecting what you have. A church never arrives at perfection. There is always room for improvement. You'll always be fine-tuning the dynamics of the group, the discipleship equipping, and the way you coach children's cell leaders.

The moment, in fact, that a church thinks it has arrived, it probably has already begun its downward spiral. John P. Kotter, business professor at Harvard University, wrote a book called *Leading Change*, in which he talks about complacency being the enemy of progress.[83] Kotter's advice is to practice gut-level honesty and to avoid a sense of complacency at all costs.

The Vine Church has excelled in their cell structure partly because they have developed a first class coaching structure for all children's cell leaders. Each children's cell leader has a coach who meets with the leader each week. Perfecting their coaching structure has taken a long, long time with many revisions along the way.

The discipleship equipping is another area that needs to be fine-tuned. Perhaps you will use the one you already have, adapting it to meet the needs of children. Or perhaps you could use someone else's equipping, like Daphne Kirk's *Living with Jesus*.[84] Or you might follow the example of the Vine Church that does some of the equipping when the children are younger but finishes the equipping after the child turns twelve.

Another area that needs to be constantly evaluated and improved is the recruitment of new workers for teaching children in the larger gatherings and the cells. New workers are always needed to replace the ones who drop out and to open new groups. Recognition of those ministering to children is an area that is frequently overlooked. Most churches need to improve in this area. And even though the leader knows his or her reward is in heaven, God tells us to appreciate those who labor among us (1 Thess. 5:12).

DON'T WAIT

Don't wait for perfection before starting your children's cell ministry. Granted, it's important to spend enough time to really capture the values and biblical foundation behind cell ministry, but then it's best to jump in and perfect the process as you move along. You'll adapt as you press ahead. God will give you insight as you walk along the path because he's more interested than you are in discipling children who will continue the discipleship process.

Chapter 10
VISION MISTAKES

When people try something new, they rarely get things right the first or second time—and often mistakes are still made after three or four more attempts. In fact, human beings grow and mature through trial and error. The key is to learn from mistakes and not to allow discouragement to take control. Proverbs 24:16 says, "For though a righteous man falls seven times, he rises again, but the wicked are brought down by calamity."

John Maxwell wrote a book called *Failing Forward*, which is an appropriate title for those prioritizing children in cell ministry.[85] Maxwell's book is a reminder that failure is the back door to success, and God will use mistakes to teach and perfect.

You will make mistakes with children in cell ministry. You will have to adjust. Just don't make the mistake of failing to try to work through the mistakes. God only asks us to move forward. He can't use us if we're passive. We only learn and grow as we go forward with a willingness to make and overcome our mistakes. Henry Cloud and John Townsend wrote an excellent book called *Boundaries*. They write,

> God's grace covers failure, but it cannot make up for passivity. We have to do our part. The sin God rebukes is not trying and failing, but failing to try. Trying, failing, and trying again is called learning. Failing to try will have no good result; evil will triumph. God expresses his opinion toward passivity in Hebrews 10:38-39: "But my righteous one will live by faith. And if he shrinks back, I will not be pleased with him." . . . Passive shrinking back is intolerable to God, and when we understand how destructive it is to the soul, we can see why God does not tolerate it.[86]

As you read this chapter, you might identify with some of the mistakes made in children's ministry. Here are a few:

NOT PRIORITIZING A CHILD'S SPIRITUAL CONDITION

Given the tender and sweet character of children, people adopt a loving and condescending attitude. This is fine as long as a child's spiritual needs are given high priority. In other words, one of the biggest mistakes is to not take the child's spiritual condition seriously.[87] Each child has particular needs that we should try to meet.

Children's cells shouldn't be turned into a game. Children have spiritual needs equivalent to those of adults. Their main need is to know Jesus. It is a real spiritual battle—the one that has to be fought for the salvation of children. It involves prayer, teaching of the Word of God, and dependence on the Holy Spirit.

Children, like adults, have powerful testimonies of salvation and use of their spiritual gifts. I heard of a group leader who asked for prayer for a friend who had a migraine headache. She asked one of the children to pray for her. "Dear Lord Jesus," prayed the child, "please take away her headache, take away the pain, and don't let her die."[88] Everybody laughed and began to explain to the child that one did not die from a migraine headache! The next day the leader telephoned to inquire how the migraine headache was. "Haven't you heard?" came the reply, "It wasn't a migraine, it was meningitis." And she did not die! Simple faith so often eludes adults, while children don't have the same obstacles.

Repentance, the new birth, and experiences of encounter with God also occur in children. But because they are children, there is the risk of minimizing those experiences, or to not give them their rightful importance.

The fact that they are children does not mean that their prayers, songs, and tears have no legitimacy. Maybe they can't articulate their experiences theologically like an adult, but that does not diminish their authenticity. Remember that Jesus placed children as a model.

Because children often speak in imaginative language, adults don't listen to what's behind their "ramblings." Because the kids have no life experience to speak of, their notion of how the world operates can range pretty far out in left field. We need to remember that children are often dreaming of a distant future that will change many times before they become older.

Yet, we do need to listen to them and affirm their dreams and visions.[89] We need to take them seriously and prepare them as disciples, like we would anyone else.

NOT TAKING THE DISCIPLESHIP PROCESS SERIOUSLY

When a child has been born again, he or she should be nurtured and mentored. His or her desire to be baptized and partake of the Lord's supper should be taken seriously. All of their faith experiences are as real as that of adults. Children need to be prepared to walk with God on a daily basis. It's easy to ignore that children, like adults, need to practice the presence of God and the spiritual disciplines. Ivy Beckwith writes,

> Many of the traditional spiritual disciplines can be practiced meaningfully by children. . . I think one of the important things about practicing meditation, and teaching our kids to practice meditation, is that it has to be done in quiet. We live in a very noisy world, and our kids are rarely quiet or in quiet. It's impossible to hear God's voice and reflect on it in noisy environments. I think there are some adults out there who don't think kids can or want to "do" silence. Well, they can do silence, and enjoy it when it is offered to them.[90]

Ralph Neighbour has concluded that the greatest pitfall facing the cell church movement is its failure to disciple children and form cells for children between the ages of five and thirteen. He writes, "Seventy-nine years ago as a five-year old child, I accepted Jesus as my Lord sitting on my father's lap. It has amazed me to meet Christian workers who think we do not need to focus on harvesting children." He goes on to say,

Our tendency is to develop home cells for young people and adults, relegating the children during cell meetings to baby sitters or viewing television. George Barna's research shows that what a person believes at age 13 is pretty much what that person will continue to believe throughout his or her lifetime. Children between the ages of 5 and 13 have a 32 percent probability of accepting Jesus Christ as their Savior. That likelihood drops to 4 percent for teenagers between the ages of 14 and 18, and ticks back up to 6 percent for adults older than 18.[91]

Many, many children don't know Jesus Christ and need to be evangelized and discipled. We need to labor for them and to recognize that Jesus wants the Church to be a mighty army to evangelize children and adults.

The church's work with parents is only one side of the equation. The church also has to work directly with the children. Some churches and pastors affirm their responsibility to contribute to the spiritual development of children but fail to back up that affirmation with time, money, and planning. The pastor who spends all of his time with adults or planning adult programs neglects a significant portion of his flock.[92]

NOT VIEWING CHILDREN AS FULL PARTICIPANTS OF GOD'S KINGDOM

Many tend to view children as receptacles into which the teacher pours knowledge about God and the Bible. It is true that information about God and Scripture is essential to growing a child's faith. Yet we need to realize that God views children as full participants in his kingdom. Jesus did not say,

"Children belong to the kingdom;" he said, "The kingdom belongs to the children" (Luke 18:15-17). They are not merely the Church of tomorrow; they are the Church of today. Adults may be older in earthly years, but their praise and worship is no higher than that of the children. The reality is that in God's eyes we are all children. We all have a father-child relationship with our Father in heaven.

Seeing children as priests of the living God, just like adults, helps empower their faith. It encourages them to see God working in their own lives. Cell groups for children are excellent vehicles for developing the priesthood of all believers, including the children.

NOT VALUING THEIR EMOTIONAL NEEDS

Many adults trivialize or discount their child's emotions and even feel justified in doing so, repeating the often used phrase, "They are just children." Some parents rationalize such indifference with the belief that concerns of children over broken toys or playground politics are petty, especially when compared to adult-size worries about things like job loss, the solvency of one's marriage, or what to do about national debt. Furthermore, they reason, children can be irrational. John Gottman writes,

> Asked how he responds to his daughter's sadness, one perplexed father answers that he doesn't respond at all. "You're talking about a four-year old," he says. Her feelings of sadness are often "based on lack of understanding of how the world works," and therefore not worth much in his estimation.[93]

Such thinking is shortsighted and misguided.

Adults should take children seriously. Those ministering to children should know and care about the little details in the lives of the children under their care. Perhaps an adult notices erratic behavior from the child. The adult needs to inquire and try to do something about it. Children are practically powerless to alter or control the world around them. Wise, sensitive adults understand that children have emotions, needs, problems, and difficult circumstances. If something is happening in the child's life that an adult can control, then it's important to try to fix it.[94]

Leaders of children's cell groups need to be perceptive and aware of what's happening both spiritually and emotionally. The authors of *The Young Child as Person* write,

> Each child selects certain things from his environment and makes them his world. A teacher needs to know what a child is including in that world. What activities does the child participate in? Who does the child play with? Who does he avoid? Why? Which children does the child look upon as helpers in his projects?[95]

Children's emotional and spiritual sides are at least as strong as their intellectual lives. They don't (or can't) hide from their feelings; so they know all about what it's like to surrender to forces that transcend their control. Children easily accept that their words are not adequate to describe thoughts and feelings; they know that real worth and importance goes beyond words.

The church often errs by not allowing children to express their feelings. Hearing and helping a child clarify his feelings creates a deeper level of understanding than only catching the verbal content. Sometimes a child's words do not communicate the true feelings beneath them.[96] The key is to realize that children have feelings and need to express them and be transparent about their lives. As families disintegrate and as moral standards become lower and lower, it's essential for cell leaders and teachers to get to know the children, find out about their backgrounds, and then minister accordingly.

NOT EQUIPPING THE CHILDREN'S WORKERS

It might appear that the church has all the workers necessary, but in almost every case, this is a mirage. There will always be new positions and new opportunities to work with children. A church needs to prepare for the future. The Elim Church is able to care for thousands of children because they have a vision to develop new children's leaders. Because the harvest of children is so continual, Elim is constantly envisioning and preparing for new leaders; they are constantly preparing to reap the harvest through new children's workers.

Cell churches don't allow "just anyone" to lead the children's cells. Children's workers need to be trained, screened, and coached. Cell churches ask all members of the church to go through the church-wide equipping, and this is also the requirement of those working with children.

Beyond the basic equipping, those leading children should know how to treat children. They need to learn how to be gentle, kind, and full of patience. Jesus said, "See that you do not look down on one of these little ones. For I tell you that their angels in heaven always see the face of my Father in heaven" (Matt. 18:10). God loves children, and those ministering to them must be careful to treat them with love and kindness. A children's worker should never threaten the child with something like "I'm going to kick you out of the room if you continue."

Those working with children should also be trained in how to deal with sick children. Sick children should not be allowed to join in the activities or even sit by themselves. The church should have a firm policy about not allowing children who appear to be ill to be in the presence of other children. Parents whose children become infected through exposure to other sick classmates are hesitant to bring them back. Those leading cell groups or working with children in the celebration services should be trained to recognize the signs of contagious diseases.[97]

NOT OBTAINING THE PROPER LEGAL PROTECTION

Churches should not allow the fear of abuse or legal nightmares to hinder them from making disciples of children. On the other hand, they must make sure that they are legally covered and doing everything to protect the children. It is important that churches have the proper insurance coverage and background checks in place. Churches need to make sure that those working with children have been screened properly and are ministering in teams of at least two people.

The pastor and the church need to have in place a child protection policy that is known, and adhered to. It's good to have a resource person in the church who is aware of the policies and will keep the protection requirements up-to-date.

REPORTING ABUSE

The pastor is a mandatory reporter of all abuse. Part of this mandatory requirement to report abuse includes:

- never telling a parent before reporting
- never questioning a minor when they tell you something
- affirming them and saying they were right to tell you

Churches must be ready and willing to report all abuse. Even if determined that the workers are not mandated by law to report the abuse, it's a good idea to do so. This responsibility includes situations in which the abuse occurs in connection with ministry activities or when it happens completely independently of them.

Workers should be trained to know the signs of abuse and be ready to report such abuse. Rarely does abuse happen in the church or in a home cell group. Abusers normally groom their victims by:

- introducing forbidden behavior such as drugs, alcohol, or pornography.
- giving a child money to create a dependency.
- excessive attention to kids; doing one-on-one activity with children.
- earning the trust of overburdened parents under the guise of showing extra concern for a troubled child.[98]

Again, abuse rarely happens during an official church activity; rather the abuser uses the trust gained during the spiritual activity to lure the child to be alone on another occasion. In these cases, it is very difficult or nearly impossible for ministry leaders to have known about the abusive behavior.[99]

When abuse is suspected, workers need to report the abuse. Choun and Lawson write, "In most states, health and education professionals are required to report suspicions of child abuse. In some locations, clergy are also required to do so.

Failure to report such cases can be punishable by fines, jail terms, or both."[100]

NEVER ALONE WITH A MINOR

All church activity should have at least two adults present. Team ministry, in fact, has biblical precedence, since leadership in the New Testament is always plural.[101] Here are some precautions:

- One adult should never be alone with a child.
- Children's workers should be qualified to teach the children what is a good touch and a bad touch. In other words, they should be ready to report abuses that they see.
- Don't allow the child to go to the bathroom alone. Always be on alert for child molesters.

These precautions might include having extra adults on hand to observe and help whenever children are gathered.[102]

BACKGROUND CHECKS

All those working with minors must be checked for their background. Bill Stout writes, "Organizations have also been found negligent if a criminal background check would have turned up a prior record of child abuse, and the checks were not conducted."[103]

A policy asking newcomers to your church to wait six months before volunteering in children's ministry is another proven precaution. This gives you time to get to know the newcomer's qualifications, and it discourages sexual predators who are only coming to your church for quick access to children.

DON'T BE PARALYZED BY FEAR

While the threats of child abuse are real, one grave mistake is being paralyzed by fear, an emotion that Satan and his demons welcome and even generate among churches and children's workers. The fear of what might happen is often the enemies' greatest tactic for paralyzing churches and discouraging ministers from discipling the next generation.

It's a lot like the person who rarely goes outside because of the fear of being murdered on the street. Yes, the media is filled with reports of murders happening every day, but the reality of being a victim is quite different. Murders are very rare when compared to the country's population and the same is true with child abuse in churches. Yes, it does happen, and churches need to do everything possible to prevent it. But they must not allow themselves to become immobilized by what might happen.

Even though governments and laws are there to protect children, they are not proactively trying to shut down Christian ministries. In fact, most cases where there have been problems, the courts have ruled that an organization cannot be expected to protect its children from bizarre or completely unforeseen types of harm. Bill Stout writes,

> In the event of a lawsuit, courts usually ask some variation of this question: Did the organization take reasonable and prudent precautions to protect the child? If the answer is a clear "yes," then your ministry will not be judged at fault for the injury."[104]

In other words, the church simply needs to make sure there are legal, reasonable, and prudent safeguards in place. But after putting those safeguards in place, make sure you press ahead with your intentions to disciple the children in cell ministry. The devil likes nothing more than to cause the ministry of the church to grind to a halt. Many pastors feel that they have enough problems in their adult ministry to even think about children's ministry. And some pastors allow perceived legal fears to hinder them from preparing children to be disciples through cell-based ministry.

You will make mistakes. You will face obstacles. But you will also prepare the next generation of ministers, provide a steady flow of leadership in your church, and tap into the most willing and ready group of people in the church—the children.

NOT PRAYING

Training, material, or legal exactitude should never be a substitute for dependence on Jesus through prayer. The reality is that children's ministry is spiritual warfare. Satan and his demonic following would prefer that the church not prioritize children. The enemy of our souls does not want to see children formed by the Spirit of God. If the church is not praying, the battle will be too fierce, the devil will deceive too readily. We must not forget the importance of prayer. It's all important.

The best remedy against fear and the best way to motivate people to get in involved in cell ministry is through prayer. In fact, the first and foremost solution to the transformation of the church and the development of children is prayer—a humble, radical crying out to God for help. Commitment to prayer allows us to rely on God himself for wisdom and direction. It teaches us to depend on him to discover the best way to develop children or get the parents involved.

Paul wrote the Colossian epistle at the end of his life, and it's noteworthy that one of his final exhortations was about prayer. He said, "Devote yourselves to prayer, being watchful and thankful" (Colossians 4:2). The Greek word for devote literally means to attend constantly. To illustrate his point, Paul uses the example of Epaphras, ". . . who is always wrestling in prayer for you, that you may stand firm in all the will of God, mature and fully assured" (Col. 4:12). Epaphras labored fervently and constantly for the believers in Colossae. We must continually cry out, "Lord, make us like Epaphras!"

Only through dedicated prayer will parents be willing to carve out time in their busy schedules and prioritize the development of their own children. Commitment to prayer is the arsenal that God has given to his entire body of believers. And it's the most important weapon God has given the Church to win souls and make disciples.

Churches—charismatic or not—that prioritize prayer realize that only God can make disciples of the next generation. It's a myth to rely on books, techniques, or even experience in developing children. Only God can provide sustained growth and protection.

This book is all about prioritizing those who don't have a voice or power in the decision making at the church level. Because prioritizing children through cell ministry is not the norm, it works best among a group of people committed to God's supernatural power that comes through prayer. Only through prayer can the church break down cultural resistance and live New Testament lifestyles in community with one another. Only through prayer and an emphasis on spirituality will members be willing to dedicate volunteer time to prepare the future generation now.

True success in cell groups and cell churches comes from God. The secret is not the cell structure, the cell order, or the cell pastor—it is the blessing of the almighty God upon the congregation. God spoke to Jeremiah saying, "But let him who boasts boast about this: that he understands and knows me, that I am the LORD, who exercises kindness, justice and righteousness on earth, for in these I delight," (Jer. 9:24). Those who lead children and develop the next generation need to possess the essential characteristic of dependence on God, along with the knowledge and practice of diligent prayer. Other leadership characteristics can help, but spirituality is the chief requirement.

Chapter 11

VISION FOCUS

We've noted in this book how much Jesus loves children, prioritizes them, and even tells us that we must become like them to enter the kingdom of God. Jesus says,

> I tell you the truth, unless you change and become like little children, you will never enter the kingdom of heaven. Therefore, whoever humbles himself like this child is the greatest in the kingdom of heaven. And whoever welcomes a little child like this in my name welcomes me. But if anyone causes one of these little ones who believe in me to sin, it would be better for him to have a large millstone hung around his neck and to be drowned in the depths of the sea (Matt. 18:3-6).[105]

After quoting the above verses, Luis Bush writes in his book, *The 4/14 Window: Raising Up a New Generation to Transform the World*,

> Have we really listened to this teaching about the place of children in the kingdom of God? It contains three truths: First children model the essence of saving faith and discipleship. Becoming like them is required in order to "enter the kingdom of heaven." Second, to "welcome a child"—that is, to accept, love, value, and respect a child—is to welcome Christ Himself! Finally, as Jesus made very clear, whoever neglects, abuses, hinders, or turns away a child from faith will face God's severe judgment.

Throughout this book, I've highlighted the importance of children, how to develop them as disciples right now, and the need to take the first steps. Yet, we must first and foremost remember to let them come, knowing their special place in God's heart.

LET THEM COME

In his earthly ministry, Jesus was always ready to accept children. He welcomed them and made time for them, even in the busiest moments of his ministry. So should we. There is only a fleeting moment before children become youth and adults, and it's during this childhood period that they are ready to learn, eager to care, and desirous of changing the world.

God blesses churches that prioritize children. A church that allows the children to come is a church with a future perspective—a church that is fulfilling the great commission and starting with those who have most time on this earth.

We've seen how IG cells provide the atmosphere in which parents can bring the whole family, talk about what they learn afterwards, and prepare the children to do ministry. CO cells allow for incredible versatility to find and disciple children throughout the city. The celebration and equipping provide the finishing touches to prepare children to become disciples.

But first we must let them come. We must hear Christ's heartbeat for the children and allow them to come to Jesus. Then our job is to nurture them and even allow them to lead us.

LET THEM LEAD

Isaiah 11:6 says, "The wolf will live with the lamb, the leopard will lie down with the goat, the calf and the lion and the yearling together; and a little child will lead them." It's the last part that captures my attention: a little child will lead them. The prophet envisions a time in the future in which children will lead the way.

Throughout Scripture we see God entrusting special truths to children or using them as his messengers. Wess Stafford, president emeritus of Compassion International, often says that when God has something really important to do, something that he couldn't entrust to adults, he uses children. He writes, "God seems to pause, run his hands together, smile warmly, and say, 'I need someone really powerful for this task. I know. . . I will use a child.'"[106]

God hides his great truths from the learned and reveals them to infants (Matt. 11:25). God has placed his love and blessing on children, and in one sense, he leads the Church through them, telling us that we must become like them and follow their humility and simple trust to even enter the kingdom of heaven.

Those churches who prepare for the future realize adult leadership will soon be passing. Pastor Keison at MCM understood this truth when he pondered why Wales, a historic place of red-hot revival, was now stagnant, spiritually dry, and filled with empty churches. When children lead and are prioritized, a church looks ahead into a bright future, one that multiplies new leaders.

LET THEM MULTIPLY

From the very beginning, God told the first humans to be fruitful and multiply (Gen. 1-7). The immediate context of Genesis is physical birth and reproduction, but this same theme is repeated in Matthew 28 when Jesus refers to spiritual rebirth and making disciples of the nations. I've often used those chapters in Genesis combined with Matthew 28 to talk about multiplying adult groups, but I was shortsighted. Adults are already in their full strength. Yes, they're wiser and more versatile, but they don't have the potential, nor the humility as children. As Luis Bush talks about in *The 4/14 Window*, the focus of our mission and attention needs to be saving and discipling the little ones.

If we can tap into a child's energy and potential, we have an entire future to deal with. In fact, some of the amazing cell churches highlighted in this book started with children in mind. In the Vine Church, Marcia Silva, caught a vision for children and never stopped propagating that vision. The Vine movement is brimming with enthusiasm as leaders from the around the world celebrate and receive training to lead more than 10,000 children's cell groups. Mario Vega realized long ago that Elim could never build enough Sunday school classes to reach the multitudes of San Salvador. They decided to take the Sunday school to the people through home cell groups.

Many other pioneers and practitioners are mentioned in this book. All of them have one thing in common: they are discipling the future generation now. These pioneers centered their resources on the most vulnerable and dependent age group, but the same group who has the most potential. Christ's commission to make disciples of the nations should remind us that children are a vital part of our attention and resources right now.

On the other hand, the discipleship process is reciprocal. In a very real sense, children disciple us. After all, unless we change and become like little children, we will never enter the kingdom of heaven. The greatest in God's kingdom, in fact, will be those who practice the humility of a child. Children teach us what greatness is all about, and in the process they show us how to truly become disciples of Jesus Christ.

Endnotes

1 Mario Vega, "Working with Children in the Cell Church," blogpost on Joel Comiskey Group on October 10, 2013.

2 Mario Vega blogged on this topic on the Joel Comiskey Group website on November 1, 2013 under the title, "Vision for Children's Cells."

3 Carolyn Osiek, Margaret Y. MacDonald, Janet H. Tulloch, *A Women's Place: House Churches in Earliest Christianity* (Minneapolis, MI: Augsburg Fortress, 2006), Kindle edition, pp. 73-74.

4 Osiek, MacDonald, Tulloch, Kindle edition, pp. 70-71.

5 John M.G. Barclay, "The Family as the Bearer of Religion in Judaism and Early Christianity," in *Constructing Early Christian Families*, Halvor Moxnes, ed. (London: Routledge, 1997), p. 76.

6 Osiek, MacDonald, Tulloch, Kindle edition, pp. 76-77.

7 Mary VanderGoot, *Helping Children Grow Healthy Emotions* (Grand Rapids, MI: Baker Book House, 1987), p. 34.

8 Lorna Jenkins, *Shouting in the Temple: A Radical Look at Children's Ministry* (Singapore: Touch Ministries International, 1999), p. 94.

9 Daphne Kirk, *Heirs Together: Establishing Intergenerational Cell Church* (Suffolk, U.K.: Kevin Mayhew LTD, 1998), p. 31.

10 I've written three books dedicated to coaching and two books which talk about coaching. I recommend these books in the following order: *How to Be a Great Cell Group Coach: Practical Insight for Supporting and Mentoring Cell Group Leaders* (Houston, TX: Touch Publications, 2003), *Coach: Empower Others to Effectively Lead a Small Group* (Moreno Valley, CA: CCS Publishing, 2008), *You Can Coach: How to Help Leaders Build Healthy Churches through Coaching* (Moreno Valley, CA: CCS Publishing, 2011), *Passion and Persistence: How the Elim Church's Cell Groups Penetrated an Entire City for Jesus* (Houston TX: Touch Publications, 2004), *From Twelve to Three: How to Apply G-12 Principles in Your Church* (Houston TX: Touch Publications, 2002). You can also read twenty-seven free articles about coaching at http://www.joelcomiskeygroup.com/articles/coaching/coaching.htm.

11 Lorna Jenkins, *Shouting in the Temple: A Radical Look at Children's Ministry*, p. 120.

12 It's common for *intergenerational groups* or *children only* cell groups to use the teaching on Sunday in the cell lesson. Since the goal is to discipleship—becoming like Jesus—the children are reminded of what they learned in their children's church or Sunday school time. In this way, the children are able to ask questions and apply the spiritual truths that were taught in the sermon. I have become increasingly convinced of the effectiveness of basing the cell lesson on the general Sunday teaching, whether that teaching is the pastor's sermon or monthly curriculum. The key is reinforcing and connecting what is taught in the larger gathering with the cell lesson.

13 Lorna Jenkins, *Shouting in the Temple: A Radical Look at Children's Ministry*, p. 120.

14 Kevin Giles, *What on Earth Is the Church? An Exploration in New Testament Theology* (Downers Grove, IL: InterVarsity Press, 1995), p. 20.

15 Daphne Kirk, "Are your children being Discipled," (Cell Group Journal, Winter 2000), p. 12.

16 Lawrence O. Richards, *A Theology of Children's Ministry* (Grand Rapids, MI: Zondervan, 1983), p. 45.

17 Child Evangelism Fellowship is a worldwide organization that has established around 3500 after-school groups in public elementary schools whose aim is to convert children as young as four to evangelical Christianity. For many years, CEF met in homes, but has more recently targeted schools.

18 Personal email from Lorna Jenkins on Sunday, June 28, 2015.

19 Lorna Jenkins, "What's Different About a Children's Cell Group," blog post on October 23, 2013 on Joel Comiskey Group.

20 Robert Banks, P*aul's Idea of Community* (Peabody, MA: Hendrickson Publications, 1994), p. 49

21 Lorna Jenkins, *Feed My Lambs: A Handbook for Intergenerational Cell Groups* (Singapore: Touch Ministries International, 1995), p. 22

22 A lot of the material in this section came from several blogs that Brian Kannel wrote on Joel Comiskey Group in May 2012: http://joelcomiskeygroup.com/blog_2/2012/05/30/our-journey-into-childrens-cells/. I've edited this material but some of the Kannel's wording is verbatim.

23 Daphne Kirk, *Reconnecting the Generations* (Suffolk, Great Britain: Kevin Mayhew Ltd., 2001), p. 39

24 Ibid, p. 33

25 As much as possible, I like to call the children's cell a fully functioning cell group, rather than just an extension of the adult cell. Yet to call it a separate cell, it's important to have someone in charge, whether that person is appointed by the cell leader or the local church

26 Erik Fish, "What Do You Do with Kids at a House Church?" on CMA Resources at https://www.cmaresources.org/index.php?q=article/what-do-you-do-with-kids_erik-fish. Posted on November 23rd, 2010. Accessed on Thursday, December 11, 2014.

27 Scottie May, Beth Posterski, Catherine Stonehouse, Linda Cannell (2005-09-15), *Children Matter: Celebrating Their Place in the Church, Family, and Community* (Eerdmans Publishing, Kindle edition), pp. 144-147

28 Kevin Walsh, *Discipline for Character Development* (Birmingham, AL: R.E.P. Books, 1991), p. 112.

29 Daphne Kirk, "Simple Remedies with Children in Cells," blogpost on March 04, 2013 on www.joelcomiskeygroup.com.

30 Holly Allen, "What Do You Do with Children in a Cell Church?" (Jan 1, 1996), Leaven: Vol. 4: Is. 3, Article 9. Available at: http://digitalcommons.pepperdine.edu/leaven/vol4/iss3/9.

31 I recommend making song sheets or projecting the words on a TV. Why?

-First-time visitors will feel uncomfortable without seeing the words.

-Some new Christians or church members don't know the worship choruses of your church.

-You'll have more liberty to sing new songs.

32 Rainey, Dennis and Barbara Rainey (2007-10-01). *Moments with You: Daily Connections for Couples* (p. 67). Gospel Light. Kindle edition.

33 Daphne Kirk, *Heirs Together: Establishing Intergenerational Cell Church*, p. 52.

34 "Our History," Accessed on Monday, August 17, 2015 at http://www.littlefalls.co.za/our-history.

35 Conversations with Robert Lay in 2015 as well as written correspondence via email. I've done dozens of seminars with Robert Lay throughout Brazil, have a copy of some of Lay's children's materials, and have witnessed churches using this material. I testify that it is excellent. Ralph Neighbour has repeatedly told me that he feels it's the best material available.

36 First Baptist Campo Grande doesn't count the children's part of the IG group as an additional cell group. They do, however, count the total number of people present in the adult cells. I encouraged the church to count the IG groups as regular cell groups when they are functioning on a weekly basis. Why? Because it truly is a cell group. A team of leaders (parents within the adult cell) are facilitating the group and there is regularity of meeting (weekly). The children are being discipled, just like the adults. It fits my definition of a cell: "3-15 people who meets weekly outside the church building for the purpose of evangelism, community, and spiritual growth with the goal of making disciples who make disciples that results in multiplication." All the cell elements are present, and I believe counting it as one of their cell groups would help the church to take their IG cells more seriously. This means that First Baptist Campo Grande would have 360 cell groups, rather than 300.

37 I was at this event and noted that probably about 30 people received a plaque/trophy for leading a cell for 25 years or more. These leaders had multiplied their cell many times in the process but continued leading even after their multiplication.

38 Mario Vega, "Working with Children in the Cell Church," blogpost on Joel Comiskey Group on October 10, 2013.

39 The Vine Church has a conference each year to promote their children's cell groups and to teach others how to implement children's cells in their churches. Some 10,000 leaders come together from all over Brazil to learn about their children's ministry. During this conference, they celebrate the "Feast of Multiplication" of children in cells in Brazil and in countries where they have the Vine Churches.

40 Here are some additional information about children's cell groups at the Vine Church:

-Video of Radical Kid's Conference with 10,000 children leaders! (https://www.youtube.com/watch?v=z0J_UamwxIw)

-Video about Vine statistics international (http://youtu.be/Myp6E_ZiXEM)

-Video about Vine statistics in Brazil Brasil(http://youtu.be/jXeL1Dj7Znk)

-Video of what the Vine does in children's ministry (https://drive.google.com/file/d/0B5MNuGWf3ppXY3ZMN3hxUUEzOGc/view)

Another video of the equipping that children go through at the Vine (https://drive.google.com/file/d/0B5MNuGWf3ppXeEp3WjFSeHFrblE/view)

41 It was my understanding that the church believes that women have more influence over CO cells because there's not the same problem of sexual abuse.

42 Neal F. McBride, *How to Build a Small-Groups Ministry* (Colorado Springs, CO: NavPress, 1995), p. 128.

43 I've seen churches teach the equipping one-on-one, one-on-two or -three, equipping after the cell group meeting, equipping during Sunday school hour, seminars, retreats, or a combination of all of them.

44 Daphne has written best-selling books on the theme of generation to generation equipping and intergenerational cell groups. Check out her resources here: http://www.daphnekirk.org.

45 Equipping cell leaders is a common feature in all cell churches. My book, *Leadership Explosion* (Houston, TX: Touch Publications, 2000) explains the entire process. My own equipping consists of five books, *Live, Encounter, Grow, Share,* and *Lead* and can be purchased at www.joelcomiskeygroup.com or by calling 1-888-511-9995.

46 Personal email sent to me on Friday, July 3, 2015.

47 If you are interested in obtaining Lorna Jenkin's material, please contact Dorcas Li at dorcas.li@gfi-singapore.org or dorcasli@singnet.com.sg . After FCBC became a G 12 church, they stopped using Jenkin's material but adopted the material from Cesar Castellano's church. However after many years, FCBC has now brought back many equipping track books that were written by Lorna Jenkins and successfully used for many years. Those books have been reprinted by Growing Families International, Singapore.

48 Lorna Jenkins, *Shouting in the Temple: A Radical Look at Children's Ministry*, p. 223

49 Lorna Jenkins, *Shouting in the Temple: A Radical Look at Children's Ministry*, p.237.

50 Personal email sent to me on Friday, July 3, 2015.

51 Robert J. Choun and Michael S. Lawson, *The Christian Educator's Handbook on Children's Ministry* (Grand Rapids, MI: Baker Books, 1998), p. 260.

52 Ivy Beckwith, *Formational Children's Ministry* (Grand Rapids, MI: Baker Book House, 2010), p. 24.

53 Robert J. Choun and Michael S. Lawson, *The Christian Educator's Handbook on Children's Ministry*, p. 261.

54 Ivy Beckwith, Formational Children's Ministry, p. 35.

55 Evelyn M. R. Johnson & Bobbie Bower, *Building a Great Children's Ministry*, Lyle E. Schaller, editor (Nashville, TN: Abingdon Press, 1992), p. 21.

56 Dr. Paul Warren and Dr. Frank Minirth, *Things That Go Bump in The Night* (Nashville, TN: Thomas Nelson Publishers, 1992), p. 63.

57 David Cohen and Stephen A. MacKeith, *The Development of Imagination: The Private Worlds of Childhood* (New York: Routledge, 1991), p. 10.

58 Delmont Morrison, "The Child's First Ways," *Organizing Early Experience, Delmont Morrison*, editor (Amityville, New York: Baywood Publishing Company, 1988), p. 10.

59 Wes Haystead, *Teaching Your Child about God: You Can't Begin Too Soon* (Ventura, CA: Regal Books, 1974), p. 57.

60 R. P. Smith, *"Where Did You Go?" "Out." "What Did You Do?" "Nothing"* (New York: Norton, 1957), pp. 70-71, 97-98.

61 Diana Shmukler, "Imagination and Creativity in Childhood: The Influence of the Family," *Organizing Early Experience*, Delmont Morrison, editor (Amityville, New York: Baywood Publishing Company, 1988), p. 88.

62 Mary VanderGoot, *Helping Children Grow Healthy Emotions* (Grand Rapids, MI: Baker Book House, 1987), p. 89.

63 Rebecca Nye (2011-12-07). *Children's Spirituality* (What It Is and Why It Matters) (Kindle Locations 280-282). Hymns Ancient and Modern, Ltd. Kindle edition.

64 Ralph Neighbour, "Avoiding Pitfalls in Children's Ministry," blogpost on October 20, 2013 on Joel Comiskey Group.

65 Rebecca Nye (2011-12-07). *Children's Spirituality* (What It Is and Why It Matters) (Kindle Locations 229-240). Hymns Ancient and Modern, Ltd. Kindle edition.

66 Mary VanderGoot, *Helping Children Grow Healthy Emotions* (Grand Rapids, MI: Baker Book House, 1987), p. 50.

67 Anna B. Mow, *Preparing Your Child to Love God* (Grand Rapids, MI: Zondervan, 1983), p. 33.

68 Ivy Beckwith, *Formational Children's Ministry* (Grand Rapids, MI: Baker Book House, 2010), p. 120.

69 Mike Sciarra, "Partnering with Parents," *Children's Ministry that Works!* (Loveland, Colorado: Group, 2002), p. 60.

70 Lawrence O. Richards, *A Theology of Children's Ministry* (Grand Rapids, MI: Zondervan, 1983), p. 269.

71 Ibid, p. 269.

72 Vernon Anderson, *Before You Teach Children* (Philadelphia: Lutheran Press, 1962), p. 48.

73 Ivy Beckwith, *Formational Children's Ministry* (Grand Rapids, MI: Baker Book House, 2010), pp.18-19.

74 Mike Sciarra, "Partnering with Parents," *Children's Ministry that Works!* (Loveland, Colorado: Group, 2002), p. 60.

75 Michael Farris, *What a Daughter Needs from Her Dad* (Minneapolis: Bethany House, 2004), p. 26.

76 Evelyn M. R. Johnson and Bobbie Bower, *Building a Great Children's Ministry*, Lyle E. Schaller, editor (Nashville, TN: Abingdon Press, 1992), p. 29.

77 Scottie May, Beth Posterski, Catherine Stonehouse, Linda Cannell (2005-09-15), *Children Matter: Celebrating Their Place in the Church, Family, and Community* (Eerdmans Publishing, Kindle edition), pp. 159-161.

78 Mike Mason, *The Practice of the Presence of People* (Colorado Springs: WaterBrook Press, 1999), p. 106.

79 The institution of marriage is sinking quickly in many nations around the world. Although the United States might be a poor example of marriage success, it does serve as a warning: In the U.S. in 2015, 41% of babies were born to single mothers. This huge percentage is 2.5 times as high as reported in 1980 and nineteen times as high as in 1940.

80 Lorna Jenkins, *Shouting in the Temple: A Radical Look at Children's Ministry*, p. 94.

81 Roger Thoman, "House Church Basics Pt. 7: What About Children?" Written on March 18, 2004 and accessed on Thursday, December 11, 2014 at http://sojourner.typepad.com/house_church_blog/2004/03/house_church_ba_3.html .

82 Everett M. Rogers, *Diffusion of Innovations*, 4th Ed. (New York: The Free Press, 1995), pp. 7-8.

83 John P. Kotter, *Leading Change* (Boston, MA: Harvard Business Press, 2012), pp. 288.

84 Daphne's equipping, along with her many other materials can be purchased here: http://www.daphnekirk.org/

85 John Maxwell, *Failing Forward* (Nashville, TN: Thomas Nelson Publishers, 2007), pp. 224.

86 Henry Cloud and John Townsend, *Boundaries,* (Grand Rapids, MI: Zondervan, 1992), pp. 99–100.

87 Mario Vega, "Mistakes When Working with Children's Cells," blog post on Joel Comiskey Group on October 24, 2013.

88 Daphne Kirk, *Reconnecting the Generations* (Suffolk, Great Britain: Kevin Mayhew Ltd., 2001), p. 23.

89 Dr. Paul Warren and Dr. Frank Minirth, *Things That Go Bump in The Night* (Nashville, TN: Thomas Nelson Publishers, 1992), p.152.

90 Ivy Beckwith, *Formational Children's Ministry* (Grand Rapids, MI: Baker Book House, 2010), pp. 105-107.

91 Ibid.

92 Robert J. Choun and Michael S. Lawson, *The Christian Educator's Handbook on Children's Ministry* (Grand Rapids, MI: Baker Books, 1998), p. 24.

93 John Gottman, *Raising an Emotionally Intelligent Child* (New York, NY: Fireside, 1997), p. 55.

94 Dr. Paul Warren and Dr. Frank Minirth, *Things That Go Bump in The Night*, p. 78.

95 Martha Snyder, Ross Snyder, Ross Snyder, Jr., T*he Young Child as Person* (New York, NY: Human Science Press, 1980), p. 101.

96 Ibid, p. 152.

97 Robert J. Choun and Michael S. Lawson, *The Christian Educator's Handbook on Children's Ministry*, p. 187.

98 Bill Stout, "Safety and Liability in Children's Ministry," *Children's Ministry that Works!* (Loveland, Colorado: Group, 2002), p. 40.

99 Ibid, p. 41.

100 Robert J. Choun and Michael S. Lawson, *The Christian Educator's Handbook on Children's Ministry*, p. 54.

101 The norm in the early church was to have a team of leaders over house churches. Paul, for example, told the leaders of the Ephesian church that the Holy Spirit had made them "overseers" of the flock (Acts 20:28). When writing to the church at Philippi, Paul greeted the congregation and, separately, the "overseers" (Phil. 1:1). When he wrote to Titus, Paul directed the appointment of elders, whom he also identified with the functions of "overseer" (Tit. 1:5-7). Whether they are designated as a "body of elders" (1 Tim. 4:14) or simply as "elders," this form of leadership was always exercised by a group of people rather than by one single individual (Acts 20:17; 1 Tim. 5:17; Tit. 1:5; James 5:14; 1 Pet. 5:1-4).

102 Bill Stout, p. 44.

103 Ibid, p. 41.

104 Ibid, p. 41.

105 Luis Bush, *The 4/14 Window: Raising up a New Generation to Transform the World* (Colorado Spring, CO: Compassion International, 2009), p. 5.

106 Wess Stafford, *Too Small to Ignore* (Colorado Springs, CO, WaterBrook Press, 2005), p 212, as quoted in Luis Bush, *The 4/14 Window: Raising up a New Generation to Transform the World* (Colorado Springs, CO: Compassion International, 2009), p. 5.

──────── Resources ────────

RESOURCES BY JOEL COMISKEY

> You can find all of Joel Comiskey's books at Joel Comiskey Group
>
> Phone: 1-888-511-9995
>
> Website: www.joelcomiskeygroup.com

Joel Comiskey's previous books cover the following topics

- Leading a cell group (*How to Lead a Great Cell Group Meeting*, 2001, 2009).
- How to multiply the cell group (*Home Cell Group Explosion*, 1998).
- How to prepare spiritually for cell ministry (*An Appointment with the King*, 2002, 2011).
- How to practically organize your cell system (*Reap the Harvest*, 1999; *Cell Church Explosion*, 2004).
- How to train future cell leaders (*Leadership Explosion*, 2001; *Live*, 2007; *Encounter*, 2007; *Grow*, 2007; *Share*, 2007; *Lead*, 2007; *Coach*, 2008; *Discover*, 2008).
- How to coach/care for cell leaders (*How to be a Great Cell Group Coach*, 2003; *Groups of Twelve*, 2000; *From Twelve to Three*, 2002).
- How the gifts of the Spirit work within the cell group (*The Spirit-filled Small Group*, 2005, 2009; *Discover*, 2008).
- How to fine tune your cell system (*Making Cell Groups Work Navigation Guide*, 2003).
- Principles from the second largest church in the world (*Passion and Persistence*, 2004).
- How cell church works in North America (*The Church that Multiplies*, 2007, 2009).
- How to plant a church (*Planting Churches that Reproduce*, 2009)
- How to be a relational disciple (*Relational Disciple*, 2010).
- How to distinguish truth from myths (*Myths and Truths of the Cell Church*, 2011).
- What the Biblical foundations for cell church are (*Biblical Foundations for the Cell-Based Church*, 2012, *Making Disciples in the Cell-Based Church*, 2013, *2000 Years of Small Groups*, 2015).

All of the books listed are available from Joel Comiskey Group
www.joelcomiskeygroup.com

Resources by Joel Comiskey

How To Lead A Great Cell Group Meeting: *So People Want to Come Back*

Do people expectantly return to your group meetings every week? Do you have fun and experience joy during your meetings? Is everyone participating in discussion and ministry? You can lead a great cell group meeting, one that is life changing and dynamic. Most people don't realize that they can create a God-filled atmosphere because they don't know how. Now the secret is out. This guide will show you how to:
- Prepare yourself spiritually to hear God during the meeting
- Structure the meeting so it flows
- Spur people in the group to participate and share their lives openly
- Share your life with others in the group
- Create stimulating questions
- Listen effectively to discover what is transpiring in others' lives
- Encourage and edify group members
- Open the group to non-Christians
- See the details that create a warm atmosphere

By implementing these time-tested ideas, your group meetings will become the hot-item of your members' week. They will go home wanting more and return each week bringing new people with them. 140 pgs.

Home Cell Group Explosion: *How Your Small Group Can Grow and Multiply*

The book crystallizes the author's findings in some eighteen areas of research, based on a meticulous questionnaire that he submitted to cell church leaders in eight countries around the world, locations that he also visited personally for his research. The detailed notes in the back of the book offer the student of cell church growth a rich mine for further reading. The beauty of Comiskey's book is that he not only summarizes his survey results in a thoroughly convincing way but goes on to analyze in practical ways many of his survey results in separate chapters. The happy result is that any cell church leader, intern or member completing this quick read will have his priorities/values clearly aligned and ready to be followed-up. If you are a pastor or small group leader, you should devour this book! It will encourage you and give you simple, practical steps for dynamic small group life and growth. 175 pgs.

An Appointment with the King: *Ideas for Jump-Starting Your Devotional Life*

With full calendars and long lists of things to do, people often put on hold life's most important goal: building an intimate relationship with God. Often, believers wish to pursue the goal but are not sure how to do it. They feel frustrated or guilty when their attempts at personal devotions seem empty and unfruitful. With warm, encouraging writing, Joel Comiskey guides readers on how to set a daily appointment with the King and make it an exciting time they will look forward to. This book first answers the question "Where do I start?" with step-by-step instructions on how to spend time with God and practical ideas for experiencing him more fully. Second, it highlights the benefits of spending time with God, including joy, victory over sin, and spiritual guidance. The book will help Christians tap into God's resources on a daily basis, so that even in the midst of busyness they can walk with him in intimacy and abundance. 175 pgs.

Reap the Harvest: *How a Small Group SysSystem Can Grow System Can Grow Your Church*

Have you tried small groups and hit a brick wall? Have you wondered why your groups are not producing the fruit that was promised? Are you looking to make your small groups more effective? Cell-church specialist and pastor Dr. Joel Comiskey studied the world's most successful cell churches to determine why they grow. The key: They have embraced specific principles. Conversely, churches that do not embrace these same principles have problems with their groups and therefore do not grow. Cell churches are successful not because they have small groups but because they can support the groups. In this book, you will discover how these systems work. 236 pgs.

La Explosión de la Iglesia Celular: *Cómo Estructurar la Iglesia en Células Eficaces* (Editorial Clie, 2004)

This book is available only in Spanish and contains Joel Comiskey's research of eight of the world's largest cell churches, five of which reside in Latin America. It details how to make the transition from a traditional church to the cell church structure and many other valuable insights, including: the history of the cell church, how to organize your church to become a praying church, the most important principles of the cell church, and how to raise up an army of cell leaders. 236 pgs.

Resources by Joel Comiskey

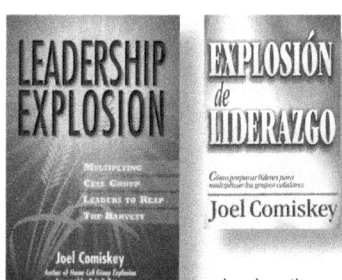

Leadership Explosion: *Multiplying Cell Group Leaders to Reap the Harvest*

Some have said that cell groups are leader breeders. Yet even the best cell groups often have a leadership shortage. This shortage impedes growth and much of the harvest goes untouched. Joel Comiskey has discovered why some churches are better at raising up new cell leaders than others. These churches do more than pray and hope for new leaders. They have an intentional strategy, a plan that will quickly equip as many new leaders as possible. In this book, you will discover the training models these churches use to multiply leaders. You will discover the underlying principles of these models so that you can apply them. 202 pgs.

FIVE-BOOK EQUIPPING SERIES

#1: Live   #2: Encounter   #3: Grow   #4: Share   #5: Lead

The five book equipping series is designed to train a new believer all the way to leading his or her own cell group. Each of the five books contains eight lessons. Each lesson has interactive activities that helps the trainee reflect on the lesson in a personal, practical way.

Live starts the training by covering key Christian doctrines, including baptism and the Lord's supper. 85 pgs.
Encounter guides the believer to receive freedom from sinful bondages. The Encounter book can be used one-on-one or in a group. 91 pgs.
Grow gives step-by-step instruction for having a daily quiet time, so that the believer will be able to feed him or herself through spending daily time with God. 87 pgs.
Share instructs the believer how to communicate the gospel message in a winsome, personal way. This book also has two chapters on small group evangelism. 91 pgs.
Lead prepares the Christian on how to facilitate an effective cell group. This book would be great for those who form part of a small group team. 91 pgs.

TWO-BOOK ADVANCED TRAINING SERIES

Coach

Discover

Coach and **Discover** make-up the Advanced Training, prepared specifically to take a believer to the next level of maturity in Christ.

Coach prepares a believer to coach another cell leader. Those experienced in cell ministry often lack understanding on how to coach someone else. This book provides step-by-step instruction on how to coach a new cell leader from the first meeting all the way to giving birth to a new group. The book is divided into eight lessons, which are interactive and help the potential coach deal with real-life, practical coaching issues. 85 pgs.

Discover clarifies the twenty gifts of the Spirit mentioned in the New Testament. The second part shows the believer how to find and use his or her particular gift. This book is excellent to equip cell leaders to discover the giftedness of each member in the group. 91 pgs.

How to be a Great Cell Group Coach: *Practical insight for Supporting and Mentoring Cell Group Leaders*

Research has proven that the greatest contributor to cell group success is the quality of coaching provided for cell group leaders. Many are serving in the position of a coach, but they don't fully understand what they are supposed to do in this position. Joel Comiskey has identified seven habits of great cell group coaches. These include: Receiving from God, Listening to the needs of the cell group leader, Encouraging the cell group leader, Caring for the multiple aspects of a leader's life, Developing the cell leader in various aspects of leadership, Strategizing with the cell leader to create a plan, Challenging the cell leader to grow.

Practical insights on how to develop these seven habits are outlined in section one. Section two addresses how to polish your skills as a coach with instructions on diagnosing problems in a cell group, how to lead coaching meetings, and what to do when visiting a cell group meeting. This book will prepare you to be a great cell group coach, one who mentors, supports, and guides cell group leaders into great ministry. 139 pgs.

Groups of Twelve: *A New Way to Mobilize Leaders and Multiply Groups in Your Church*

This book clears the confusion about the Groups of 12 model. Joel dug deeply into the International Charismatic Mission in Bogota, Colombia and other G12 churches to learn the simple principles that G12 has to offer your church. This book also contrasts the G12 model with the classic 5x5 and shows you what to do with this new model of ministry. Through onsite research, international case studies, and practical experience, Joel Comiskey outlines the G12 principles that your church can use today.

Billy Hornsby, director of the Association of Related Churches, says, "Joel Comiskey shares insights as a leader who has himself raised up numerous leaders. From how to recognize potential leaders to cell leader training to time-tested principles of leadership—this book has it all. The accurate comparisons of various training models make it a great resource for those who desire more leaders. Great book!" 182 pgs.

From Twelve To Three: *How to Apply G12 Principles in Your Church*

The concept of the Groups of 12 began in Bogota, Colombia, but now it is sweeping the globe. Joel Comiskey has spent years researching the G12 structure and the principles behind it.

From his experience as a pastor, trainer, and consultant, he has discovered that there are two ways to embrace the G12 concept: adopting the entire model or applying the principles that support the model.

This book focuses on the application of principles rather than adoption of the entire model. It outlines the principles and provides a modified application which Joel calls the G12.3. This approach presents a pattern that is adaptable to many different church contexts.

The concluding section illustrates how to implement the G12.3 in various kinds of churches, including church plants, small churches, large churches, and churches that already have cells. 178 pgs.

The Spirit-filled Small Group: Leading Your Group to Experience the Spiritual Gifts.

The focus in many of today's small groups has shifted from Spirit-led transformation to just another teacher-student Bible study. But exercising every member's spiritual gifts is vital to the effectiveness of the group. With insight born of experience in more than twenty years of small group ministry, Joel Comiskey explains how leaders and participants alike can be supernaturally equipped to deal with real-life issues. Put these principles into practice and your small group will never be the same!
This book works well with Comiskey's training book, **Discover.** It fleshes out many of the principles in Comiskey's training book. Chuck Crismier, radio host, Viewpoint, writes, "Joel Comiskey has again provided the Body of Christ with an important tool to see God's Kingdom revealed in and through small groups." 191 pgs.

Making Cell Groups Work Navigation Guide: A Toolbox of Ideas and Strategies for Transforming Your Church.

For the first time, experts in cell group ministry have come together to provide you with a page reference tool like no other. When Ralph Neighbour, Bill Beckham, Joel Comiskey and Randall Neighbour compiled new articles and information under careful orchestration and in-depth understanding that Scott Boren brings to the table, it's as powerful as private consulting! Joel Comiskey has an entire book within this mammoth page work. There are also four additional authors.

Passion and Persistence: How the Elim Church's Cell Groups Penetrated an Entire City for Jesus

This book describes how the Elim Church in San Salvador grew from a small group to 116,000 people in 10,000 cell groups. Comiskey takes the principles from Elim and applies them to churches in North America and all over the world. Ralph Neighbour says: "I believe this book will be remember as one of the most important ever written about a cell church movement! I experienced the passion when visiting Elim many years ago. Comiskey's report about Elim is not a pattern to be slavishly copied. It is a journey into grasping the true theology and methodology of the New Testament church. You'll discover how the Elim Church fans into flame their passion for Jesus and His Word, how they organize their cells to penetrate a city and world for Jesus, and how they persist until God brings the fruit." 158 pgs.

The Church that Multiplies: *Growing a Healthy Cell Church in North America*

Does the cell church strategy work in North America? We hear about exciting cell churches in Colombia and Korea, but where are the dynamic North American cell churches? This book not only declares that the cell church concept does work in North America but dedicates an entire chapter to examining North American churches that are successfully using the cell strategy to grow in quality and quantity. This book provides the latest statistical research about the North American church and explains why the cell church approach restores health and growth to the church today. More than anything else, this book will provide practical solutions for pastors and lay leaders to use in implementing cell-based ministry. 181 pgs.

Planting Churches that Reproduce: *Planting a Network of Simple Churches*

What is the best way to plant churches in the 21st century? Comiskey believes that simple, reproducible church planting is most effective. The key is to plant churches that are simple enough to grow into a movement of churches. Comiskey has been gathering material for this book for the past fifteen Years. He has also planted three churches in a wide variety of settings. Planting Churches that Reproduce is the fruit of his research and personal experience. Comiskey uses the latest North American church planting statistics, but extends the illustrations to include worldwide church planting. More than anything else, this book will provide practical solutions for those planting churches today. Comiskey's book is a must-read book for all those interested in establishing Christ-honoring, multiplying churches. 176 pgs.

The Relational Disciple: *How God Uses Community to Shape Followers of Jesus*

Jesus lived with His disciples for three years and taught them life lessons as a group. After three years, he commanded them to "go and do likewise" (Matthew 28:18-20). Jesus discipled His followers through relationships—and He wants us to do the same. Scripture is full of exhortations to love and serve one another. This book will show you how. The isolation present in the western world is creating a hunger for community and the world is longing to see relational disciples in action. This book will encourage Christ-followers to allow God to use the natural relationships in life—family, friends, work relationships, cells, church, and missions to mold them into relational disciples.

You Can Coach: *How to Help Leaders Build Healthy Churches through Coaching*

We've entitled this book "You Can Coach" because we believe that coaching is more about passing on what you've lived and holding others accountable in the process. Coaching doesn't require a higher degree, special talent, unique personality, or a particular spiritual gift. We believe, in fact, that God wants coaching to become a movement. We long to see the day in which every pastor has a coach and in turn is coaching someone else. In this book, you'll hear three coaches who have successfully coached pastors for many years. They will share their history, dreams, principles, and what God is doing through coaching. Our hope is that you'll be both inspired and resourced to continue your own coaching ministry in the years to come.

Myths & Truths of the Cell Church: *Key Principles that Make or Break Cell Ministry*

Most of the modern day cell church movement is dynamic, positive, and applicable. As is true in most endeavors, errors and false assumptions have also cropped up to destroy an otherwise healthy movement. Sometimes these false concepts caused the church to go astray completely. At other times, they led the pastor and church down a dead-end road of fruitless ministry. Regardless of how the myths were generated, they had a chilling effect on the church's ministry. In this book, Joel Comiskey tackles these errors and false assumptions, helping pastors and leaders to untangle the webs of legalism that has crept into the cell church movement. Joel then guides the readers to apply biblical, time-tested principles that will guide them into fruitful cell ministry. Each chapter begins with a unique twist. Well-known worldwide cell church leaders open each chapter by answering questions to the chapter's topic in the form of an email dialogue. Whether you're starting out for the first time in cell ministry or a seasoned veteran, this book will give you the tools to help your ministry stay fresh and fruitful.

Biblical Foundations for the Cell-Based Church

Why cell church? Is it because David Cho's church is a cell church and happens to be the largest church in the history of Christianity? Is it because cell church is the strategy that many "great" churches are using?

Ralph Neighbour repeatedly says, "Theology must breed methodology." Joel Comiskey has arrived at the same conclusion. Biblical truth is the only firm foundation for anything we do. Without a biblical base, we don't have a strong under-pinning upon which we can hang our ministry and philosophy. We can plod through most anything when we know that God is stirring us to behave biblically.

Making Disciples in the Cell-Based Church

The primary goal of the church is to make disciples who make disciples. But how is the church supposed to do that? This book answers that question. Dr. Comiskey explains how both cell and celebration (larger gathering) work together in the process of making disciples. In the cell, a potential disciple is transformed through community, priesthood of all believers, group evangelism, and team multiplication. The cell system ensures each leader has a coach and that training happens. Then the cells gather together to worship and grow through the teaching of God's Word. This book will help you understand why and how to become a church that prioritizes discipleship.

What others are saying: I've read all of Joel Comiskey's books, but this one is his best work yet. I'm looking forward to having all of our pastors, coaches, cell leaders and members read this book in the near future. *Dr. Dennis Watson, Lead Pastor, Celebration Church of New Orleans*

I am so excited about Joel Comiskey's new book, Making Disciples in the Twenty-First Century Church. Joel has unpacked discipleship, not just as an endeavor for individuals, but as the critical element for creating a church community and culture that reproduces the Kingdom of God all over the earth. *Jimmy Seibert, Senior Pastor, Antioch Community Church*

Like Joel's other books, this one is solidly biblical, highly practical, wonderfully accessible and is grounded in Joel's vast research and experience. *Dr. Dave Earley, Lead Pastor, Grace City Church of Las Vegas, Nevada*

2000 Years of Small Groups: A History of Cell Ministry in the Church

This book explores how God has used small groups throughout church history, specifically focusing on the early church to the present time. God not only established the early church as a house to house movement, but he also has used small groups throughout church history. This book chronicles the small group or cell movement from Jesus all the way to the modern day cell explosion. Themes include:

- Small Groups In Biblical History
- Small Groups In Early Christian History
- Small Groups and Monasticism
- Small Groups During the Pre-Reformation Period
- Luther and Small Groups
- Martin Bucer and Small Groups
- The Anabaptist Movement
- Puritan Conventicles
- Pietism
- The Moravians
- The Methodists
- Modern House Churches
- Small Groups in North America
- The Modern Day Cell Church

This book will both critique the strengths and weaknesses of these historical movements and apply principles to today's church.

INDEX

A
abuse, 99, 106, 109, 115, 183, 184, 185, 186, 201
Alberto, Luis, 114
Almeida, Marcelo, 106
Alves, John Paul, 108
Antioch Community Church, 217

B
Baquisimieto, 38, 104
Beckham, Bill, 17, 214
Beckwith, Ivy, 133, 178, 202, 203, 205
Bird, Warren, 22
Bower, Bobbie, 135, 202, 204
Bowman family, 64
Brazil, 6, 18, 39, 50, 51, 84, 86, 87, 106, 112, 113, 114, 116, 200, 201
Breder, Gilson, 87
Bush, Luis, 49, 192, 194, 206

C
Carrillo, Keison, 36
cell, 4, 208, 209, 210, 211, 212, 213, 214, 215, 216, 217
Celyce, 160
Cho, Paul Yonggi, 55
Choun and Lawson, 133, 184
City Harvest, 126
Cloud, Henry, 176, 204

CO groups, 20, 92, 93, 96, 98, 99, 102, 105, 106, 107, 108, 109, 110, 111, 113, 115, 116, 117, 171
Cusco, Peru, 92, 114

D

David Cho, 217
Dirk Willems, 119
discipleship equipping, 119, 161, 171

E

Einstein, 41
Elim, 214
Elim Church, 14, 18, 39, 44, 92, 95, 182, 198, 214, 219
Encounter retreat, 105, 108, 111, 112, 117, 131, 132
equipping, 4, 17, 34, 38, 39, 40, 43, 50, 56, 84, 88, 93, 99, 102, 103, 104, 105, 108, 111, 112, 113, 116, 117, 118, 119, 120, 121, 122, 123, 124, 125, 126, 127, 128, 131, 132, 139, 140, 142, 143, 146, 150, 151, 153, 156, 160, 161, 162, 171, 172, 182, 193, 201, 202, 204, 211

F

Faith Community Baptist Church, 17
FCBC, 17, 40, 46, 56, 81, 127, 130, 131, 140, 165, 170, 202
Ferris, Michael, 156
First Baptist Church in Campo Grande, 39

G

Gabriel, 102, 103
Goiania, 106, 111, 116

I

icebreaker, 16, 17, 57, 61, 68, 70, 71, 73, 92, 93, 98, 103, 110, 116, 124, 170
IG groups, 17, 18, 20, 40, 56, 58, 59, 61, 62, 63, 68, 70, 71, 73, 80, 82, 83, 84, 86, 87, 88, 89, 92, 93, 94, 102, 110, 170, 200
intergenerational cell groups, 16, 58, 59, 60, 67, 77, 198, 201

J

Jenkins, Lorna, 6, 15, 17, 38, 40, 44, 46, 52, 56, 58, 81, 89, 127, 131, 140, 165, 170, 198, 199, 202, 204
Johnson, Evelyn M. R., 135, 202, 204

K

Kannel, Brian, 59, 77, 151, 199
Khong, Laurence, 17, 56
Kids' Slot, 62, 82, 83, 86, 151
Kirk, Daphne, 7, 15, 17, 18, 38, 42, 51, 56, 60, 61, 70, 74, 89, 122, 172, 198, 199, 200, 205
Kole, Andre, 74
Korea, 215
Kotter, John P., 171, 204

L

Lay, Robert, 84, 85, 88, 151, 200
Legal Protection, 183
Leonel, 96, 97

Index

Lewis, C. S., 133
Little Falls Christian Centre, 80, 81
Living with Jesus, 122, 172
Luis, 49, 50, 51, 114, 192, 194, 206

M

Marcia Silva, 6, 46, 48, 106, 107, 149, 194
Maxwell, John, 175, 204
McBride, Neil F., 120
MCM, Misión Cristiana para el Mundo, 36, 104
Müller, George, 139

N

Neighbour, Ralph, 17, 55, 56, 80, 89, 140, 178, 200, 203, 214, 217, 220
Noah, 33, 34
Nye, Rebecca, 139, 203

P

Pastor Aldezir, 88
Phelps, Michael, 30
Pilot Group, 169
Prayer, 156, 157
prototype, 169, 170

R

Richards, Lawrence, 52

S

Sciarra, Mike, 152, 156, 203, 204

Shouting in the Temple, 17, 40
Shuey, Jacob, 77
Silva, Aluizio, 46, 48, 106, 149
Silva, Marcia, 6, 46, 48, 106, 107, 149, 194
Stevens, Giles, 116
Storytelling, 133, 135

T

Townsend, John, 176, 204

V

VanderGoot, Mary, 35, 198, 203
Vega, Mario, 14, 49, 95, 150, 194, 197, 201, 204
Vine Church, 6, 18, 39, 44, 48, 92, 106, 108, 111, 115, 116, 117, 131, 132, 149, 165, 171, 172, 194, 201

W

Wales, 36, 104, 150, 194
Weitsz, Harold, 80
Welcome, 71, 76, 93, 100, 122
Witness, 75, 76, 93
Worship, 47, 73, 76, 93, 98, 100, 130

Y

York Alliance Church, 18, 58, 77
youth cells, 16, 19, 39, 83, 106, 111, 115, 145

Z

Zschech, Darlene, 73

www.ingramcontent.com/pod-product-compliance
Lightning Source LLC
LaVergne TN
LVHW020927090426
835512LV00020B/3242